Praise for *The New York Times* Bestselling
Faith and Politics

"With passion, clarity, and common sense, John Danforth has given us a gift: a lucid, powerful book that is at once reflective and instructive. By candidly writing about his own unusual pilgrimage through what Roger Williams called 'the wilderness of the world and the garden of the church,' Danforth—priest and politician—sheds light on the complexities and ambiguities of religion and politics. Jesus once told his followers that 'in this world ye shall have tribulation, but be of good cheer,' and, reading Danforth, one is heartened anew that if we conduct ourselves with humility and a sense of history, we shall find fresh cause to be of good cheer as we face the storms of the present."

—Jon Meacham, editor of *Newsweek* and author of *American Gospel: God, the Founding Fathers, and the Making of a Nation*

"It's impressive stuff. . . . Danforth appeals for the kind of ecumenical cooperation . . . that requires people of different beliefs to work together, without a preset program or claim to possess the absolute truth. 'God calls us to be faithful without handing us a political agenda,' he writes."

—*Seattle Post-Intelligencer*

"Former Senator John Danforth is in many ways a political dinosaur. That is unfortunate because the world would be a better place if people like him were not nearly extinct. . . . While it's not clear how effective the book will be in changing minds, those who care about improving the state of national affairs should welcome it as an important contribution to our political dialogue."

—*The Washington Times*

"This stirring book—part political memoir, part sermon, part moral plea—reminds us again why the remarkable Jack Danforth has become one of the most respected voices in American political life. His thoughtfulness, deep wisdom, and simple decency radiate from every page, and leave one at the end with rare hope that through commitment, faith and politics can ultimately enrich, and not corrupt, one another."

—Harold Hongju Koh, Dean, Yale Law School

"[A] wise and intelligent book . . . In a time when mean-spirited political polemics are practically a cottage industry, Danforth's book provides a welcome call for moderation, understanding, and kindness."

—*Daily Herald* (Provo, Utah)

"This is an important book that challenges each of us to participate thoughtfully in American politics."
—Nancy Kassebaum Baker, U.S. Senator, Kansas, 1978–1997

"Danforth oozes sincerity and good sense as he excoriates 'Christian conservatives' . . . for corrupting religious doctrine on reproduction and marriage and inappropriately inserting it in government. Conceding that he's an imperfect human being who sometimes failed as a student, husband, father, lawyer, minister and senator, Danforth comes across as a welcome paragon of virtue." —*Publishers Weekly*

"Jack Danforth has become a brave and treasured voice in America. Here in this compelling book, he challenges the Republican Party—the party he has loved and served well—to loosen its ties to the Christian Right so that religion can once again be a reconciling, and not a divisive, force in our society. This book and its author are a modern-day profile in courage."
—David Gergen, Professor and Director of the Center for Public Leadership, The Kennedy School of Government, Harvard University

"Danforth's is a welcome voice of reason and moderation during a time of divisive and polarizing rhetoric. As priest and politician he ably sets forth the deeper truths of the Christian tradition with clarity and compassion and applies them to the issues of our time."
—Retired Presiding Bishop Frank Griswold, Episcopal Church

"Heed the call of this certain trumpet! No one speaks with more clarity, honesty or sincerity than my old friend Jack Danforth. When things would get rough in the U.S. Senate, he was the guy we would send off to negotiate our way out of the tough problems with the troops on the other side of the aisle. Heed this thoughtful and provocative message. He always gave his very best. He again does so here."
—Alan Simpson, U.S. Senator, Wyoming, 1979–1997

PENGUIN BOOKS

FAITH AND POLITICS

John Danforth is an ordained Episcopal priest, a former three-term U.S. senator (R-MO) and former U.S. ambassador to the United Nations. In 2001, President Bush appointed Danforth as special envoy for peace in Sudan, where he worked to broker a peace agreement that, in 2005, ultimately ended the twenty-year civil war.

FAITH *and* POLITICS

How the "Moral Values" Debate Divides America
and How to Move Forward Together

SENATOR JOHN DANFORTH

Penguin Books

PENGUIN BOOKS

Published by the Penguin Group

Penguin Group (USA) Inc., 375 Hudson Street, New York, New York 10014, U.S.A.

Penguin Group (Canada), 90 Eglinton Avenue East, Suite 700, Toronto,
Ontario, Canada M4P 2Y3 (a division of Pearson Penguin Canada Inc.)

Penguin Books Ltd, 80 Strand, London WC2R 0RL, England

Penguin Ireland, 25 St Stephen's Green, Dublin 2, Ireland
(a division of Penguin Books Ltd)

Penguin Group (Australia), 250 Camberwell Road, Camberwell,
Victoria 3124, Australia (a division of Pearson Australia Group Pty Ltd)

Penguin Books India Pvt Ltd, 11 Community Centre,
Panchsheel Park, New Delhi – 110 017, India

Penguin Group (NZ), 67 Apollo Drive, Rosedale, North Shore 0632,
New Zealand (a division of Pearson New Zealand Ltd)

Penguin Books (South Africa) (Pty) Ltd, 24 Sturdee Avenue,
Rosebank, Johannesburg 2196, South Africa

Penguin Books Ltd, Registered Offices:
80 Strand, London WC2R 0RL, England

First published in the United States of America by Viking Penguin,
a member of Penguin Group (USA) Inc. 2006
Published in Penguin Books 2007

10 9 8 7 6 5 4 3 2 1

Copyright © John Danforth, 2006
All rights reserved

ISBN 0-670-03787-7 (hc.)
ISBN 978-0-14-311248-8 (pbk.)
CIP data available

Printed in the United States of America
Set in Janson Text
Designed by Spring Hoteling

In memory of my brother Don

CONTENTS

Contents

PREFACE

On the Sunday before election day 2006, churchgoers throughout Missouri heard pulpit exhortations on the most controversial proposition that would appear on the state's ballot that Tuesday: the legality of early-stage stem cell research. Depending on the church, the pastor chose one side of the issue for the sermon. A Methodist minister in St. Louis County reminded parishioners of their religious duty to relieve suffering and heal the sick, thereby supporting the morality of the research. Roman Catholic churches played a videotaped message featuring Archbishop Raymond Burke telling them it was immoral to destroy human life, even if life was in the form of cells in petri dishes that would never be implanted in the wombs of potential mothers.

Sectarian engagement in the politics of stem cell research had commenced well before the week of the election, and it would not end with the closing of the polls. The debate had raged for months, and after a close election authorizing stem cell research to proceed (passing by a margin of nearly fifty thousand votes out of two million cast), the controversy continues, both in Missouri and throughout the nation. A group called Missourians Against Human Cloning wrote Missouri pastors asking them to organize voter registration drives and "get out the vote" campaigns in their churches. In January 2007, stem cell supporters received an e-mail advising them how to contact members of Congress of their denominations and urge them to support legislation that would expand research on a national level. Support and opposition, at least as officially expressed in church publications and pronouncements, has largely broken along denominational lines. In Missouri, Roman Catholic, Southern Baptist, and many conservative evangelical churches strongly opposed the ballot proposition. A committee of the United Methodist Church of Missouri, the Episcopal Church of Western Missouri, and the Rabbinical Association of Kansas City took positions supporting embryonic stem cell research.

How can it be that people of strong religious faith, even people who follow the same Lord, can come to diametrically opposing and vehemently held convictions of God's will on the same issue? That is the question Lincoln raised in his Second Inaugural Address on an issue even more bitterly divisive than stem cell research: slavery. Even then, when he believed so strongly in his position, he refused to identify his own mind with the mind of God. As the war raged, Lincoln said of the two sides:

Both read the same Bible, and pray to the same God; and each invokes His aid against the other. It may seem strange that any men should dare to ask a just God's assistance in wringing their bread from the sweat of other men's faces; but let us judge not that we be not judged. The prayers of both could not be answered; that of neither has been answered fully. The Almighty has His own purposes.

Because it did not espouse wedge issues or advance a specific agenda, the Second Inaugural Address was not what today we would think of as faith-based politics. But it is the clearest statement I know of how Christians should go about engaging in politics. It is a statement of humility and charity that Lincoln thought essential for the healing of a broken nation, which builds to this famous conclusion:

> With malice toward none; with charity for all; with firmness in the right, as God gives us to see the right, let us strive on to finish the work we are in; to bind up the nation's wounds; to care for him who shall have borne the battle, and for his widow, and his orphan—to do all which may achieve and cherish a just and lasting peace, among ourselves, and with all nations.

In the stem cell research debate, both sides would agree that there has been an abundance of malice as well as certainty about possessing God's truth, each side pointing to the other as the wrongdoer. As cochair of the Missouri campaign to support the research, I am most familiar with the excesses of the proposition's opponents. Campaigning in conservative southwest Missouri, former Republican presidential candidate Alan Keyes said of those on my side of the controversy: "God hates you." In another instance he called the Stowers Institute, a highly regarded medical research organization in Kansas City, "Worse than a Nazi death camp." Referring to my ordination in the Episcopal Church, one e-mailer told me, "You are a disgrace to any form of Christianity. . . . You are a devil disguised as a minister."

As election day drew closer, the issue of stem cell research became increasingly entangled in Missouri's race for the United States Senate. Shoring up his base of conservative Christians, Republican incumbent Jim Talent announced that he intended to vote against the ballot proposition, stating his position in a manner most likely to appeal to anti-research activists. He equated early stage stem cell research with reproducing fully developed, cloned human beings, a universally abhorrent notion expressly prohibited in the ballot proposition, and he repeatedly said that he did not want to be walking down the street one day and see himself coming the other way.

Meanwhile, Democratic candidate and eventual winner Claire McCaskill strongly supported stem cell research, gaining the support of noted actor and Parkinson's disease victim Michael J. Fox, who appeared in a television commercial supporting McCaskill and stating his hope for cures that stem cell research might produce. Fox's support for McCaskill and its linkage with the stem cell issue received added notoriety when conservative talk show host Rush Limbaugh lampooned the Fox commercial and sarcastically mimicked the symptoms of Parkinson's disease.

After seeing the Fox commercial and film clips of Limbaugh's offensive performance, I assumed that Fox had helped McCaskill and that backlash against Limbaugh would seriously hurt Talent, but the consequences turned out to be quite different from what I expected. The effect of the commercial was to make the stem cell issue much more closely identified with the Senate campaign, especially in the minds of many Republican voters. To them, being a loyal Republican had come to mean being an opponent of early-stage stem cell research since the issue was being used against their candidate. Moreover, at national, state, and local levels, the Republican party made the stem cell issue its own. The Republican National Committee contributed money to Missourians Against Human Cloning, and the Missouri Republican party paid for a mailing that said, "The liberal Democrats seek to destroy life in the name of research." In the weeks before the election, public and especially Republican support for the ballot proposition fell dramatically. In mid-September, two thirds of all decided voters and half of the decided Republicans supported early-stage stem cell research. On election day, the margin of victory had declined to 2 percent, with Republican support falling to less then one in three voters.

Opposition to early-stage stem cell research became the defining political issue in Missouri, but nationally, the controversy over same sex marriage remained the favored election year means of rallying the conservative base. Votes in both the Senate and the House to define marriage as only between a man and a woman fell predictably and pitifully short of the two-thirds majority necessary to amend the U.S. Constitution, but did serve to put Republicans on record as being overwhelmingly opposed to same sex marriage. In November 2006, the ballots in eight states contained propositions against same sex marriage, with the issue failing only in Arizona.

In the summer of 2006, Congress fell one Senate vote short of adopting a Constitutional amendment on another "hot button" election-year issue: an authorization of power to Congress to prohibit the desecration of the American flag. In both the House and the Senate, more than 90 percent of Republicans supported the amendment. However intensely one may feel about the emotionally charged issues of same sex marriage and desecration of the flag, these do not rank with the war in Iraq, terrorism, and the future of the economy as among the most urgent matters to confront the nation. But however peripheral they are to real world concerns, they had the election year value of gaining political points for one party and against the other.

Despite ginned up votes on same sex marriage and the flag and strong opposition to early-stage stem cell research, some conservatives such as Richard Viguerre complained that Republicans lost the 2006 election because they had not gone far enough to placate the party's conservative base. In fact, the base did hold for Republican candidates. In Missouri, evangelical Christians voted overwhelmingly for Jim Talent. Nationally, exit polls showed that 71 percent of white evangelical voters supported Republicans. The problem for Republicans in 2006 was not that the religiously conservative base defected, it was that moderates who had previously supported the party decided that they no longer were able to do so. It was not so much that centrist voters turned toward the Democrats, but rather that they turned away from the Republicans.

In a *Wall Street Journal* interview after the election, New York Senator Chuck Schumer, who had chaired the Democratic Senatorial Campaign Committee, admitted that the vote had been more a repudiation of President Bush than an endorsement of his own party. In Schumer's words, "I'd say 75 percent of this election was about people's opinion of the president, and 25 percent was about what Democrats would do."

In the election, the highly unpopular war in Iraq was the most important issue before the country, but voters did not express a determination to shift from the president's policies to a new position on the war articulated by the Democrats. In fact, the Democrats failed to articulate a coherent position on the war, and expressed instead a wide range of ideas depending on who was doing the speaking. The month after the election, a *USA Today/Gallop Poll* showed that while less than one in five respondents had "a great deal" of confidence in the president to do the right thing in Iraq, only 14 percent had confidence in Democratic Congressional leaders.

My own explanation of what the president called "a thumpin'" in the 2006 election is that Republicans had gone so far in their effort to present a hard-edged image in order to appeal to their conservative base that they appeared mean spirited and extreme in the eyes of nearly everyone else. In short, Republicans have managed to transform themselves from the sunny optimism of Ronald Reagan into a party that is harsh, unattractive, and increasingly unpopular.

Although President Bush had fashioned an immigration policy that would make it possible for many of the 12 million illegal immigrants in America to become guest workers or to progress toward citizenship, Republicans as a party emphasized law enforcement, deportation, and construction of a prisonlike wall along our border with Mexico. This may have seemed a fine strategy for fanning the enthusiasm of nativists, but the Republican share of the Hispanic vote fell from 40 percent in 2004 to 30 percent in 2006.

The campaign of incumbent Republican Senator George Allen in Virginia symbolized the harsh image of his party. In a campaign appearance in rural Virginia, Allen called a dark skinned university student, a Hindu who had been born in the United States, "macaca" (a kind of monkey), and added, "Welcome to America and the real world of Virginia." Allen's comment, intended for the white rural audience to which he was speaking, received wide-spread notoriety throughout the country. Allen lost his lead in the campaign, lost the election, and, by a one-seat margin, Republicans lost control of the Senate.

After the election, another Virginia Republican, Congressman Virgil H. Goode Jr., followed the political model created by Senator Allen. Goode attacked the use of the Koran in a ceremonial swearing-in ceremony by a newly elected Congressman who is a Muslim. In a letter, Goode urged his constituents to "wake up" or there would "likely be many more Muslims elected to office and demanding the use of the Koran."

Thomas Frank's book *What's the Matter with Kansas?* documents the ascendancy of the Christian right in the Republican Party of Kansas, a movement characterized by an emphasis on opposition to abortion and the teaching of the biblical account of creation in public schools as an alternative to evolution. The movement met strong resistance in 2006, first in the September primary election when two moderate candidates for the State Board of Education defeated creationist incumbents, then in November when two former Republicans who had switched parties were elected to statewide offices as Democrats. One of the two, Mark Parkinson, who was elected lieutenant governor, had been chair of the Kansas Republican Party. The other, Johnson County prosecutor Paul Morrison, defeated incumbent Attorney General Phill Kline by the landslide margin of 58–42 percent. In his anti-abortion zeal, Kline had subpoenaed the medical records of women and girls who had sought abortions.

In June 2006, along with former White House Chief of Staff Leon Panetta and former Senator Tom Daschle, I participated in a forum at the Naval Post Graduate School in Monterey, California. The audience consisted mainly of young navy and marine officers, many of whom had served one or more tours of duty in Iraq. As it happened, the forum occurred on the same day the Senate commenced its debate on the proposed constitutional amendment on same sex marriage. During the question and answer period, one of the officers stood and identified himself as having served in Iraq. In a voice heavy with anger he asked, "With our country at war, and with so much going on in the world, I'd like to ask what the Senate thinks it's doing spending time debating same sex marriage?" I don't recall the answer our panel gave that young officer. It was probably something on the order of, "That's politics." What I do recall is the expression on the face of the questioner and the tone of his voice. He had risked his life for his country, and he was fed up with the state of politics which harps on divisive issues at the expense of addressing real problems.

As I toured America after the hardcover publication of this book, I encountered similar attitudes many times. The crowds were large and encouraging, as though they had been waiting for someone to say what they had been thinking: that our politics have become far too polarized, to the point of being dysfunctional, that few people seem to be speaking to or for the center, that most politicians and talk show pundits are inflaming the passions of people on the fringes.

A lesson of the 2006 election is the same message I heard from that young officer in Monterey, California, and what I witnessed repeatedly in the fall of 2006. Americans are catching on to wedge issue politics, and turning against positions and statements that seem hateful. At least for the time being, this has meant the decline of the Republican Party. The outpouring of affection and respect in response to the death of Gerald Ford showed that for many of us, simple decency is more important than agreement on any issue. Politicians who do not adjust to changes in public attitudes will not succeed for very long. This recognition accounts for the speedy if temporary expressions of bipartisanship that followed the 2006 election, with President Bush and various congressional leaders as well as aspiring presidential nominees expressing a new intent to work together across party lines. It was a change in tone, if not in substance, but in today's bitterly divided politics, changes of tone are important.

Many people have expressed to me a sense of powerlessness and resignation about the present state of American politics. They doubt that there is much they can do to change things. But the truth is that they are changing things. Witness the rush by politicians to appear less strident after the 2006 elections. Of course, this is a temporary political response to a public outcry. So, all the more reason to sustain the outcry.

The argument in this book is that much of the bitterness in today's politics is caused by people who believe they are acting in the name of God. I am convinced that most Americans do not want it to be so. In various forums during the past year, I have said that America cannot be divided on the basis of religion. In this country, we are all in this together. It is an applause line. We know it to be true. We feel it passionately. Everyday we read the papers and watch television and learn that people in Iraq and elsewhere kill each other in the name of religion. We do not want this to happen here. But in America, some people use religion for political reasons, and they use it to divide us. So a politician named Alan Keyes says of people with whom he disagrees, "God hates you." I believe Americans will turn against hateful religion as they turn against hateful politics. Sure, the self-righteous will hang on to their judgmentalism, but others will turn away in revulsion. It will be an ironic result for those who pronounce that they are trying to win the world for Christ.

So often, religious people seem angry and hateful when they engage in politics. They become the energetic drivers of the wedge issues that split us apart. It is important to ask whether the way we conduct ourselves is truly the way our Lord calls us to witness to the world. Lincoln didn't think so. He thought we should proceed with the nation's business in humility and without malice and with charity. In so thinking, Lincoln understood the Gospel. The Gospel is not wedge issues and smug certainty and hate. The Gospel is the good news of God's kingdom—a large and embracing kingdom that welcomes all sorts of people, even those with whom we never agree, a communion with God who loves us and forgives us and calls us to fellowship with each other.

John C. Danforth
St. Louis, Missouri

He also told this parable to some who trusted in themselves that they were righteous and regarded others with contempt: "Two men went up to the temple to pray, one a Pharisee and the other a tax collector. The Pharisee, standing by himself, was praying thus, 'God, I thank you that I am not like other people: thieves, rogues, adulterers, or even like this tax collector. I fast twice a week; I give a tenth of all my income.' But the tax collector, standing far off, would not even look up to heaven, but was beating his breast and saying, 'God, be merciful to me, a sinner!' I tell you, this man went down to his home justified rather than the other; for all who exalt themselves will be humbled, but all who humble themselves will be exalted."

—LUKE 18:9–14

(New Revised Standard Version;
all citations have been taken from this
version unless otherwise noted)

FAITH *and* POLITICS

ARE CHRISTIANS
RECONCILERS OR DIVIDERS?

At eight o'clock each Wednesday morning, a dozen or so senators gather in an interior room on the first floor of the United States Capitol for the weekly prayer breakfast. It is an intimate hour together, with no public or media present. The senators are Republicans and Democrats, liberals and conservatives. Some are regular in their attendance; others, like myself, come only occasionally. After breakfast, the leader for the day's meeting, who was chosen the previous week, speaks for five to ten minutes on a subject of his or her choice, then opens discussion to the other senators. At the end of the hour, the leader asks a colleague to offer a closing prayer.

Senators who attend the Wednesday breakfast are from a variety of religious traditions, so the discussions are neither narrowly sectarian nor heavily theological. Instead, they tend to be quite personal, touching on life experiences of the sort that bind diverse senators together. One prayer breakfast discussion I led was about the physical exhaustion of demanding work. As my text, I used the feeding of the five thousand, where the disciples, who had hoped for some time off from their ministry in a quiet place, found themselves feeding, then cleaning up after a large crowd. Another was on the embarrassment of being wrong, where I described Jonah's feeling of humiliation when, after he had prophesied its destruction, God spared Nineveh. Because they are common to everyone, certainly to all members of the Senate, feelings of exhaustion and embarrassment are the kinds of subjects appropriate for discussion at a prayer breakfast. Not discussed at these meetings are the contentious issues of the day, where members are divided by party or political philosophy or regional interests. Fighting among one another over those issues is the everyday life of senators. An hour after leaving the prayer breakfast, members will be in committee meetings wrangling about taxes or spending or how to confront terrorism. Politics is contentious. But for a brief time each week, religion brings otherwise combative senators together.

As demonstrated by the Senate prayer breakfasts, religion has the capacity to draw people together. But it can also be a powerful force that drives people apart. In the Middle East, Iraq, Sudan, the former Yugoslavia and Northern Ireland, and many other places in the world, religion has been so divisive that people have killed one another, believing they were doing the work of God. In the United States, religion has been used at times to justify violence, but it has not led us to full-scale sectarian warfare. In recent times, however, its interjection into politics has made religion a divisive force in our national life.

Are Christians Reconcilers or Dividers?

Throughout our history, the challenge to America's government has been to hold together in one nation people of different interests and, increasingly, members of different religions, ethnicities and races. In the eighteenth century, the framers of the Constitution struggled to accommodate both mercantile and agricultural interests, as well as states with relatively large and small populations. So they created a system of government in which competing interests would be represented in the two houses of Congress, and people of every point of view would be able to participate in choosing their government. With the influx of immigrants and the emancipation of slaves in the nineteenth century, the enfranchising of women and the civil rights movement of the twentieth century, and Hispanic immigration, the feminist movement and increased awareness of gays in recent decades, we have become a more diverse country, both in fact and in our self-perception. The task of holding ourselves together, so brilliantly addressed by our forebears in the eighteenth century, is no less important today, and far more complex.

The framers of the Constitution, particularly James Madison, were well aware of the power of religion to split a nation apart. America's early colonists had come from Europe, which had known religious conflict for centuries. Some colonies and states in America, before adoption of the Constitution, imposed taxes on people regardless of their faith to support one denomination or another. In Virginia, Madison and Thomas Jefferson had led the effort to abolish taxes that supported religion. In his *Commentaries on the Constitution of the United States*, written in 1883, Supreme Court chief justice Joseph Story described America before the Constitution: "In some states, Episcopalians constituted the predominant sect; in others, Congregationalists; in others Quakers; and in others again, there was a close numerical rivalry among contending

---

sects. It was impossible that there should not arise perpetual strife and perpetual jealousy on the subject of ecclesiastical ascendancy, if the national government were left free to create a religious establishment."

So the Constitution of the United States provided that, at the federal level, religion and government should be separate. There would be no religious test for holding public office. The government would not establish religion, nor would it interfere with the right of the people to practice their faiths freely. Nothing could prevent religious people from participating in the affairs of politics. Indeed, that would be their constitutional right. But government would not be identified with religion, and religion would not be tainted by government.

In recent years, the wisdom of our founding fathers has been challenged as the Republican Party has identified itself with the political agenda of Christian conservatives. For several decades, Christian conservatives such as the Reverend Pat Robertson, the Reverend Jerry Falwell, Ralph Reed and, more recently, Dr. James Dobson have been active participants in American, and particularly Republican, politics, focusing their attention mainly on the issue of abortion. But in recent years, they have moved beyond a single issue to endorse an expanded political agenda.

Followers of the Reverend Jerry Falwell have distributed a bumper sticker bearing the slogan "Vote Christian," thereby conveying the clear message that there is a Christian way to vote as opposed to a non-Christian or anti-Christian way to vote. There is no need for the bumper sticker to spell out the details. The agenda of the Christian Right is well known. It is to oppose abortion, early stage stem cell research and gay marriage, and to advocate the display of the Ten Commandments in courthouses and the teaching of intelligent design in public schools.

Are Christians Reconcilers or Dividers?

When I arrived in Washington in January 1977, I was in the philosophical center of a broad range of Republican senators. To my left were people many Republicans today would call liberals: Jacob Javits of New York, Clifford Case of New Jersey, Edward Brooke of Massachusetts and Lowell Weicker of Connecticut. To my right were conservative stalwarts, including Barry Goldwater of Arizona, Strom Thurmond of South Carolina, Jesse Helms of North Carolina and John Tower of Texas. Then there were the senators who, with me, were somewhere in the center of our party, people like Howard Baker of Tennessee, Bob Dole and his Kansas colleague Jim Pearson. Of course, such diverse Republicans had differences of opinion on various issues, but we respected each other and we respected our differences. A set of core beliefs that nearly all Republicans shared held us together. We were internationalists who believed that America had a responsibility to be a force of strength and leadership in a world then threatened by the Soviet Union. We supported an engaged foreign policy, a strong national defense and free trade. We thought that legislators should create the law and that judges should interpret it. We believed in limited government, in keeping taxes low and the burden of regulation light, and we thought that many of government's decisions should be made close to the people, at the state or local levels, not in Washington. I recall Jacob Javits, one of our most liberal Republicans, saying that ours was the pro-business party. I think that was a fair statement. We thought that more economic growth would occur, more jobs would be created and more opportunity would exist if the private sector thrived than if the federal government grew. These were, and I think still are, the beliefs Republicans hold in common.

Throughout my time in the Senate, abortion was an issue on which Republicans did not agree. And I remember one brief period of time when we heatedly debated the subject of prayer in public schools. But by and large, religion was not a political subject in those years. Certainly, our party had no religious agenda. In those years, we would have found the notion that people should "vote Christian" at least strange and probably offensive.

Since that time, the breadth of the Republican Party has narrowed. Gone are Javits, Case and Brooke; gone are Baker, Dole and Danforth. The band of Republican senators most people would call moderate now numbers a half dozen or so, and many would say good riddance, for as our party has narrowed its breadth, it has increased its strength. In 1977, I was one of only thirty-nine Republicans in the Senate, and our party was an insignificant minority in the House of Representatives. Now we have a majority in both houses of Congress.

This improved electoral status has occurred as the Republican Party has identified itself with the Christian Right, a development starkly exemplified by the government's extraordinary intervention in the case of Terri Schiavo. Responding to the demands of prominent Christian conservatives, Republican leaders rushed legislation through Congress in a frantic effort to keep a woman hooked up to a feeding tube, despite the findings of Florida courts that she was in a persistent vegetative state and had previously evinced a will not to be kept alive artificially. President George W. Bush flew from his Texas ranch to Washington on Air Force One to sign special legislation transferring jurisdiction of the Schiavo case to the federal courts. By intervening in the life and death decision of a specific individual, by transferring government power from the state level to the federal level and by conferring on a federal court jurisdiction to overrule a state court, Republican leaders gladly abandoned principles that for decades had bound their party together in order to meet the demands of Christian conservatives. They accomplished this feat with extraordinary ease. It did not even require a recorded vote in the Senate, where each member would have registered agreement or disagreement with the legislation in a manner the public could see. It was done by voice vote, and with the exception of John Warner of Virginia, no Republican member of the Senate raised the slightest objection to the proceedings.

And why should they object? Why argue with success? This is the point most frequently made by people who justify the union of the Republican Party with the Christian Right: it works. It produces electoral victory. The traditional Republican Party, they say, was a loser. The thirty-nine senators who congenially represented a broad party in 1977 were far short of a majority. Successful politics, they say, requires building coalitions, so it is good strategy to build a coalition of traditional Republicans who share views about fiscal and foreign policies and those who have become Republicans because the party advances their religious agenda. They reason that without the numbers of voters and the energy of Christian activists, Republican ideas about taxes, spending and regulation would not prevail.

But this is not a coalition of traditional Republicans and the Christian Right in the nature of a merger of equals. This is the takeover of the Republican Party by the Christian Right. That is the significance of the Terri Schiavo case. It was the total victory of Christian conservative activism over broadly shared Republican principles, a victory won with no resistance from traditional Republicans.

A modern mantra of Republican politics is "We have to appeal to our base," and by "base" is meant the Christian Right. So before elections, Republican strategists say that they have to turn out the base. When there is a battle over a Supreme Court nomination or over important legislation, they say they have to energize the base. Indeed, single-minded attention to the base has become the central strategy of the Republican Party. But the more determined the effort to please the base, the more difficult the effort becomes. As Christian conservatives have increased in importance to the Republican Party, they have been more demanding of the party.

The Christian Right has championed a set of divisive issues that test the fealty of politicians. Often called wedge issues, their purpose is to split the country apart. Politicians who vote for the wedge issues know that they will win the support of the Christian Right. Politicians who vote against them can expect the opposition of the Christian Right. One of the wedge issues, outlawing early stage stem cell research, is currently of great importance in that, if successful, it would block the search for cures of terrible diseases. Another, abortion, has retained its function as a wedge, even though the passage of more than three decades since *Roe v. Wade* has largely settled the matter, both in the courts and in public opinion. Other issues—opposition to gay marriage and the use of religious displays and observances on government property—are of little intrinsic importance except as wedges. In each case, the issue energizes the base by pitting the "people of faith" against their enemies. The Christian Right's strategy of splitting apart the American people has worked.

As I am writing this, two items have crossed my desk that illustrate how the interjection of religion into politics can turn ugly. Stem cell research is a live issue in Missouri that will be decided by voters later in the year. Donn Rubin, who is Jewish, chairs the Missouri Coalition for Lifesaving Cures, which supports stem cell research. I have been a very visible spokesman for the Coalition, and have appeared in television ads saying that attempting to cure fatal diseases such as cancer and ALS is consistent with my pro-life position. On December 18, 2005, the *Columbia Daily Tribune* published a letter to the editor written by a Baptist attacking "Donn Rubin's anti-Christian bigotry." As the letter to the editor reached me, the following e-mail arrived from a man in St. Charles, Missouri:

> I am dismayed to hear you proclaim your "pro-life" voting record in one breath and to support the willful destruction of human life for the sake of stem cell research in the next. These two positions are contrary to one another, and you, of all people, should realize that. I suggest you look to the Catholic Church for the definition of what it means to be truly "pro-life." Your mediocrity with respect to the "pro-life" movement sends confusing signals to people of faith. In the words of our Creator, "thou shalt not kill." I don't know what part of that statement could be deemed unclear to an Episcopal minister! No matter what so-called good may come from research involving stem cells, it will always cost a life to save a life. No matter how much suffering may need to be endured, the relief of the suffering at the expense of another's life is not a decision placed in the hands of man.
>
> Jack, I voted for you every time I had the chance. I am sorry to say that had I known your true feelings about "pro-life" issues, I most likely would not have.

Christian liberals have lagged behind conservatives both in developing their own political agenda and in capturing a political party. But a similar potential for divisiveness is shared by the Left and the Right. In October 2005, the Washington National Cathedral hosted a conference on progressive Christian values, which the sponsors of the conference intended to counter the efforts of the Christian Right. The invitation to the conference began in positive terms, but note how quickly it slipped into stridency. It stated that the purpose of the conference was "to work as a united front for social justice, and publicly disavow those on the Right who have attempted to co-opt the name of the Church in America." "To work . . . for social justice" is certainly a positive objective, consistent with the teachings of Christianity. To "publicly disavow those on the Right" is the repudiation of people, not the pursuit of a cause.

In his recent book, *God's Politics*, Jim Wallis, an evangelical Protestant, rightly says that God is neither a Republican nor a Democrat, but then he proceeds to set out a political agenda that is by any lights liberal and is, in his view, religiously and politically "correct." Deeply religious people come to different conclusions about how faith should influence public policy. Some committed Christians conclude that their religious beliefs guide them toward conservatism. Others, like Jim Wallis, are politically liberal. The problem is not that Christians are conservative or liberal, but that some are so confident that their position is God's position that they become dismissive and intolerant toward others and divisive forces in our national life. The tendency toward theocracy is not monopolized by the Christian Right, and it is no advance to supplant the self-confident religious agenda of the Right with a religious agenda of the Left. To do so is to say to the conservatives, "Your basic approach is good, but your politics are bad." The problem of American politics is not the different positions people take—disagreeing on positions is the nature of politics. The problem is the divisiveness that makes civil discourse, much less reasonable compromise, so difficult today. Wedge issues split us apart, and when the wedges are driven from two directions at the same time, the split becomes even more forbidding.

That religion is now a divisive force in American political life doesn't mean that in order to avoid fracturing the country, religious people should stay out of political controversies and attend only to the personal side of religion. Some faith groups—the Mennonites, for example—have chosen the course of disengagement from public life. But many people of faith believe that politics is a religious as well as a civic duty. Tradition supports that conviction. Religious people have engaged with government since Moses confronted Pharaoh. One of the books of the Bible is called Judges. Two are called Kings. That is government. Acting for God, the prophet Samuel anointed Saul and David kings of Israel. In the Old Testament, God was the ultimate ruler, and kings answered to God. As God's agents, the prophets told kings where to go and where not to go; which battles to fight and when to surrender; what to build and when; and how to treat the poor, the fatherless, the widows and the aliens. And when kings did not do as they were told, the prophets, again acting for God, confronted them and meted out punishment. The idea of incompatible realms of religion and government is not supported in the Old Testament.

Nor is it a tradition of Christianity, not since Constantine established Christianity as the religion of Rome. In our own time, Christians, believing they were furthering the demands of their faith, have championed a variety of political positions—not just the conservative agenda of the Right but also opposition to war and the death penalty, and support for civil rights, environmental protection and increased assistance to the poor.

Faith and Politics

The question is not whether people of faith should engage in politics, but how we go about doing so. Beyond the obvious choices of whether we are liberals or conservatives, Republicans or Democrats, is a more basic decision, one that is more consequential to our common life than how we might align ourselves on the issues of the day. It is whether, in the practice of our religion, we are a divisive or a reconciling force in our country. Religion is now a divisive force in American politics, but that is not to say that it should be so. As we relate our religious faith to our politics, we can choose whether we are reconcilers or dividers.

To a degree, our choices will reflect our individual temperaments. Some people like nothing more than a good fight, and what better to fight about than the combination of religion and politics? When I was in high school, there was nothing more fun for me than heated political arguments with my classmate John Rava. He was a Democrat. I was a Republican. Most kids enjoy sports. I enjoyed arguments. Yet John and I were friends. I think most people who like politics enjoy arguments. But the nature of politics today is different from arguments among friends. It is the no-holds-barred nastiness that we witness, for example, in battles over the confirmation of Supreme Court nominees. In the midst of the fiercest struggles, with their wedge issues and extreme rhetoric, Christians are attacking their opponents, not for their policies, but, as in the case of Donn Rubin, for alleged "anti-Christian bigotry."

As some people are temperamentally combative, others are naturally good natured, even many who are in the competitive world of politics. They enjoy the give-and-take of good arguments, but they conduct themselves with restraint and understand the importance of mutual respect in resolving differences. More than conflict, they enjoy fellowship—the opportunity to come together in common space—regardless of differences. These, I think, are the people who attend the weekly Senate prayer breakfast. It is not an occasion of deep theology, but of close relationships, where religion is not the wedge that drives them apart, but the glue that binds them together.

The problem with temperament is that it is a matter of feeling, good feeling or bad feeling, and it is given to change. The most confrontational person one moment can be the most congenial person the next, and vice versa. Whether religion is a divisive force or a reconciling force depends, in part, on our individual temperaments. But it should rest on something more substantial than the shifting sands of our own moods. So we should consider not just how we happen to feel, but what our religion tells us about divisiveness and reconciliation. Should religion split us apart, or should it hold us together?

As is often the case, we can find different texts in the Bible to support conflicting propositions. In the New Testament, this is the case with respect to whether Christianity is a divisive or a reconciling religion. A case for divisiveness can be made by pointing to Matthew 10:34–36, where Jesus says, "Do not think that I have come to bring peace to the earth; I have not come to bring peace, but a sword. For I have come to set a man against his father, and a daughter against her mother, and a daughter-in-law against her mother-in-law; and one's foes will be members of one's own household."

However, as the passage continues, it is clear that Jesus is speaking of the primacy of love for him over every competing allegiance, and is not advocating divisiveness for its own sake: "Whoever loves father or mother more than me is not worthy of me; and whoever loves son or daughter more than me is not worthy of me; and whoever does not take up the cross and follow me is not worthy of me. Those who find their life will lose it, and those who lose their life for my sake will find it" (Matthew 10:37–39).

By far, the more prevalent message in the New Testament urges reconciliation. In John 17, the High Priestly Prayer, Jesus prays for the unity of his followers "that they may be one." Unity is a theme in Paul's epistles, which were written to hold together fracturing churches of his time. Notably, in 2 Corinthians 5:19, Paul wrote, "[I]n Christ, God was reconciling the world to himself . . . entrusting the message of reconciliation to us." The theme of reconciliation receives special attention in Ephesians. The Epistle to the Colossians tells us that in Christ "all things hold together."

If Christianity is supposed to be a ministry of reconciliation, but has become, instead, a divisive force in American political life, something is terribly wrong and we should correct it. I think there are two aspects to what is wrong: first, our certainty that our political agenda must be God's agenda, and second, our ineffectiveness in proclaiming the message of reconciliation.

OUR CERTAINTY

If the Christian Right lacks anything, it is not certainty. There is no doubt what the Reverend Jerry Falwell means when he urges his followers to "Vote Christian." He has in mind voting for particular candidates and ballot propositions that support his political agenda. In this line of thinking, voting for a candidate who favors legalized abortion or gay marriage would not be voting Christian. During the 2004 political campaign, certain Catholic bishops underscored their agenda by stating that Catholic candidates who supported legalized abortion would not be welcome to receive Communion.

The certainty with which some Christians identify their political agenda with their religion is not supported by the Gospels, where Jesus said almost nothing about government. The sole example of his directly addressing the connection between believers and government is his response to the Pharisees when they tried to trap him with a question about paying taxes to Caesar. Jesus's response, "Render to Caesar the things that are Caesar's, and to God the things that are God's," does not mean, as it is sometimes interpreted, that the realms of God and government are so distinct that there is no connection between the two. As Jews steeped in the theocratic emphasis of the Old Testament, neither Jesus nor his interrogators would have believed that religion and politics are entirely different spheres. Indeed, Jesus's answer to the Pharisees was that support for the government by paying taxes, even support for the occupying power of Rome, was the responsibility of faithful people.

Where Jesus broke from the Old Testament tradition was not in his opposition to government, but in his refusal to specify how government should act. He did not follow the prophetic example of confronting kings and telling them what to do. And aside from telling people to pay taxes, he did not leave instructions on how citizens should relate to government, much less how to vote. In sum, the creation of a political agenda is the work of some Christians, but it was not the work of Christ.

Jesus's lack of specificity with regard to politics does not mean that the New Testament leaves us without any guidance as to public issues. The commandment that we love our neighbors as ourselves and the compassion of Jesus for the poor speak to the entirety of life, including our politics. They suggest political strategies that are consistent with the love commandment, strategies that would be supported by liberal Christians. Similarly, Saint Paul's admonitions that we control our base instincts and obey people in authority express a moral concern championed by conservative Christians. What Christians struggle to apply in their political lives are demanding but broad commands to be loving people who care for those in need as well as moral people who restrain their worst impulses. So the New Testament informs the way Christians approach politics, but that is not the same as creating an agenda. What we lack is a set of rules that tells us with specificity what political positions we should take and what candidates we should support. Jesus lets us figure that out for ourselves.

Whether religion is a divisive or a reconciling force depends on our certainty or our humility as we practice our faith in our politics. If we believe that we know God's truth and that we can embody that truth in a political agenda, we divide the realm of politics into those who are on God's side, which is our side, and those with whom we disagree, who oppose the side of God. This is neither good religion nor good politics. It is not consistent with following a Lord who reached out to a variety of people—prostitutes, tax collectors, lepers. If politics is the art of compromise, certainty is not really politics, for how can one compromise with God's own truth? Reconciliation depends on acknowledging that God's truth is greater than our own, that we cannot reduce it to any political platform we create, no matter how committed we are to that platform, and that God's truth is large enough to accommodate the opinions of all kinds of people, even those with whom we strongly disagree.

———

The indispensable requirement of a ministry of reconciliation is humility. It is the recognition that our attempts to be God's people in our politics are, at best, good faith efforts, subject to all the misjudgments and mixed motives that characterize human behavior. We are seekers of the truth, but we do not embody the truth. And in humility, we should recognize that the same can be said about our most ardent foes.

OUR INEFFECTIVENESS

Christians have a choice between reconciliation and divisiveness. Those who have chosen the latter course are getting all the attention. They are the talking heads of television, the subjects of magazine articles, the forces in American political life. In getting media attention, they have the advantage of clear positions, certainty that they possess the truth and the natural attraction of a confrontational style. By contrast, people seem boring who believe that the ministry of Christians is reconciliation. In writing an opinion piece for the *New York Times*, I thought for some time about the best word to describe the reconciling view of Christianity, and I could come up with nothing better than "moderate." How dull can you get? What was remarkable was the enthusiastic response the column received, despite the wimpy heading given it by the *Times:* ONWARD MODERATE CHRISTIAN SOLDIERS. It was as though, for the first time, someone had said there was a respectable alternative to the Christian Right. Of course, it was not the first time. Jim Wallis, for example, has been a very public voice for Christian liberalism. But on the whole, conservatives have drowned out their moderate brethren, so the column in the *Times* was widely heralded as unusual if not unique. We have not been effective in proclaiming our position.

The best advice to preachers preparing sermons is "Tell 'em what you're going to tell 'em, tell 'em, and tell 'em what you told 'em." In other words, stick to the point and don't be afraid of repetition. Moderate Christians have failed to follow that advice to the point of being oddly silent in response to the Christian Right. It is time for a clear statement of what we believe, a statement we repeat relentlessly and a statement that expresses the strength of our convictions:

- We believe in a large God, a transcendent God, a God who cannot be shrunken by political activists and stuffed into their own agendas.
- We believe that no one should presume to embody God's truth, including ourselves. We acknowledge that our political programs, however prayerfully inspired, are no more than our best efforts to be faithful to God, and that we should pursue them with humility.
- We believe that God's truth is expansive enough to embrace conflicting opinions, even on hot-button issues, even of people with whom we vehemently disagree.

Christians who espouse the ministry of reconciliation should express themselves clearly and forcefully as the alternative to those who favor divisiveness. They should preach reconciliation from their pulpits, by pronouncements issued from their hierarchies and conventions, from their great cathedrals and places of worship, by frequent statements to the media, and by messages understood and expressed by people in the pews. Christians today are not conveying a clear message of reconciliation. It is time to do so.

———

If we preach reconciliation, it is important that we practice what we preach. It would be hypocrisy to preach reconciliation where faith touches politics while we practice exclusiveness in our denominations. Divided Christianity is a scandal, clearly contrary to Christ's High Priestly Prayer "that they may be one," and clearly contrary to Paul's teaching that "we all attain to the unity of the faith." It belies any effort of Christians to be ministers of reconciliation to a fractured world. In my own tiny Episcopal Church, people who are convinced that they possess God's truth, especially with regard to the ordination of gays, have broken away and formed their own miniscule denominations. No doubt, Episcopalians hold strong opposing positions on this very controversial subject, but the Episcopal Church, historically able to embrace a variety of opinions on a range of subjects, is broad enough to hold together people on both sides of this issue.

In my home town of St. Louis, what began as a dispute over the control of finances between a parish church and the Catholic archdiocese has escalated to the point of excommunication of the parish's priest and governing board, and the archbishop's announcement that the parish is no longer part of the Catholic Church.

In describing the kingdom of God, Jesus told a story about a king who invited guests to a great dinner. When they declined the invitation, the king persisted to the point of sending servants into the streets of the town to compel anyone they could find to come to the dinner so that his house would be filled. It is a story illustrating an inviting God and an accessible kingdom. In John's Gospel, Jesus said, "In my Father's house are many rooms"—very large rooms—in the King James Version, "mansions." The image is of a Lord who is preparing a place for us in a welcoming space where there are a lot of different people. The passage is about the world to come, yet it is not only about the next life. In the Lord's Prayer, we ask that the kingdom of heaven be established on earth.

If the kingdom of God is spacious, how dare church leaders take it upon themselves to rope off these large rooms and establish crannies for some while booting out the others? Yes, Jesus told Peter, ". . . whatever you bind on earth will be bound in heaven, and whatever you loose on earth will be loosed in heaven" (Matthew 16:19). But I do not think Jesus intended a church that is more focused on loosing than on binding.

Ecumenical discussions among ecclesiastical hierarchies are so ponderously slow that I have little hope that they will accomplish much, at least not with the urgency required for an effective witness of reconciliation to a dangerously fracturing world. So I believe that the ministry of reconciliation will be led more by the members of the flock than by the shepherds. At the least, ordinary Christians should make it clear that church leaders do not speak for them if they advocate exclusivity and divisiveness, within Christianity and to the world at large. Christians can be more than a countervoice to the dividers. They can embody the ministry of reconciliation by their own ecumenical and interfaith activities. They can take an interest in other religions and participate in religious observances that are not their own. And they can make it clear that the Eucharist is not the exclusive possession of one denomination or another. The altar is God's table, and it should be open to all God's people.

Whether religion is a reconciling or divisive force in America depends on the degrees of certainty or humility with which we claim its truths to be our own. If we are convinced that our opinions on social and political questions are the law of God, then people who oppose our opinions become opponents of God. If, in contrast, we recognize the limits of our own understanding of God's truth, while acknowledging that our opponents are trying, as we are, to do God's will, we are able to be ambassadors of reconciliation. In that case, our faithfulness in politics depends less on the content of our ideology than on how we view ourselves and treat each other. Faith in politics has more to do with the way faithful people approach politics than with the substance of our positions.

CHRISTIAN LOVE
AND PRACTICAL POLITICS

I had been in the Senate maybe a year or two when George Will graciously accepted my invitation to tape a half-hour television program to be broadcast in Missouri. At the time, I hardly knew George, although I later got to know him much better and have kept in contact with him since I left the Senate. We share an intense interest in baseball, although George, as the world knows, is a fan of the Cubs, the historic rival of my beloved Cardinals. Sally and I have the privilege of being godparents of George's daughter, Victoria.

We are, roughly, contemporaries. In the late 1970s, when we taped the broadcast, George was young for his trade, and a highly respected columnist and television personality. I was a new, on-the-make senator, impressed with myself and eager to impress both George and my constituents. The plan was for George to meet me in the reception room just off the floor of the Senate, from where we were to proceed to the Senate's radio and television recording studios in the basement of the Capitol. By the time of my retirement in 1994, senators had the benefit of two recording studios, the second being in the Hart Senate Office Building. Also, there were broadcasting facilities near the Senate Gallery on the third floor of the Capitol. All this was to serve the broadcast needs of the one hundred members of the Senate.

In my mind, the time and place of the scheduled meeting with George could not have been more auspicious, as I was engaged in floor debate on some long-since-forgotten issue. That the issue is long-since-forgotten is part of the story. I envisioned the taping being necessarily delayed due to my involvement in the debate, with George Will whiling away his time in the Senate Gallery, overcome by the significance of what I was doing. Or as a fallback fantasy, I imagined bustling importantly into the reception room, breathlessly apologizing for being tied up with Senate business.

The Gallery scene never took place, but I did manage the bustle into the reception room, where I instantly told George about the critical matter of state I had been debating. Although that critical matter was not quite critical enough to warrant a place in my memory, I have a clear recollection of George's reaction as I was telling him about it. I would not call it rudeness, because George is not a rude person, but it was, to say the least, deflating. I would describe it as dismissive boredom, or a courteous way of saying "Ho hum." What I had thought terribly significant was, to a person with a perspective on government, not significant at all.

I am sure I was disappointed by George's restrained response to my efforts on the Senate floor. In my mind, I deserved no less than his wondrous acclaim. But the disappointment of the moment in no way affected my own esteem, either for myself or for the justice of my Senate causes, especially in those early years.

Why do I tell this story on myself? I do so because a ministry of reconciliation requires a degree of humility that is lacking in many politicians, and was surely lacking in me. It is difficult to reach out to others when puffed up about the importance of one's own cause. I wish I could say the episode with George Will was a rare exception, but other instances come too readily to mind. Take, for example, a battle with the great Russell Long over the taxation of oil royalties.

Russell was the Democratic chairman of the Finance Committee, and I was the committee's junior Republican. He was one of the most powerful members of the Senate. I was a freshman member of the minority party, highly dependent on the cooperation of the chairman if I was to accomplish anything in his committee. For six terms he had represented Louisiana in the Senate, a state with considerable offshore oil reserves, which it leased to producers in exchange for substantial royalties on the production.

Middle Eastern countries had dramatically increased the cost of oil, causing price increases in the United States that hurt consumers but greatly benefited American oil companies. President Carter supported a windfall profits tax to capture some of the oil companies' unexpected gain for the federal government. Like most Republicans, I was not enthusiastic about the idea of a windfall profits tax, but I reasoned that if there were such a thing, it should apply not only to private producers of oil, but to states fortunate enough to be in coastal areas with oil deposits—states that were receiving their own windfalls. So I proposed an amendment to the bill that would impose the tax on state royalties. That commenced a knock-down, drag-out fight between Chairman Long and the most insignificant member of his committee; a fight that lasted for weeks, that took place during meetings of the Finance Committee and in back rooms of the Capitol; a fight that eventually reached the Senate floor; a fight in which I absolutely believed that my cause was just; and a fight which, from the beginning, I had absolutely no chance of winning. Zero.

Russell Long had his own way of talking to his Senate colleagues. He would drape his wrist on your shoulder, come very close to you, often with his lips about three inches from your ear, and speak in low, usually cheerful and very persuasive tones. For me, the single most enjoyable aspect of serving in the Senate was dealing with Russell. But the windfall profits tax controversy was not the high point of our relationship.

One Friday afternoon, senators interested in the tax gathered in a room in the Capitol to discuss the schedule for the following week. Russell was present, of course, and I was there, carrying on as usual about state royalties, repeating myself for what must have seemed the thousandth time. When the meeting ended, Russell came up to me, draped his wrist on my shoulder, and with his characteristic smile said, "In about fifteen years, I think you will be a great senator, but for now, you're the most obnoxious person I've dealt with in the thirty years I've been here." True to the enormous esteem in which I held myself and my causes, I took that as a compliment.

It takes 51 votes to pass an amendment on the Senate floor. My month or more of intense effort produced 18. That is pathetic. That is a rout, a humiliation. More than a quarter of a century later, I ask myself why I became so embattled in such a losing effort, especially since the only predictable result would have been to spoil my relationship with Russell. Fortunately, that did not happen, as he was not one to hold grudges. In fact, I think he enjoyed the contest. But I did not know Russell that well at the time, and had little experience with his generosity of spirit. If I had been rational, and not caught up in myself, I would have believed that in picking a fight with Russell Long on a matter important to his state, I had everything to lose and nothing to gain.

The only explanation for my behavior is that I was absolutely certain that the taxation of state royalties was a colossally important issue, a matter of great principle, and that I was right and Russell Long (and, as it turned out, eighty-one other senators) were wrong. In short, I was carried away with myself, just as I had been when I bustled into the Senate Reception Room to greet George Will.

Not to dispute Russell Long's claim that I was the most obnoxious person to serve in the Senate over a span of thirty years, but I think that, to say the least, I was in good company. The Senate is designed to allow one hundred individuals to push their own agendas relentlessly; to keep the Senate in session when everyone else wants to go home; to speak endlessly, well after the point has been made; to refuse consent to proceed with the day's business—in short, to be pains in the neck. There is something called a hold. This is a senator's threat to filibuster a bill or a presidential nomination if the majority leader brings it to the floor. It is possible to break a filibuster by invoking cloture, but the process for doing that is so time consuming and the press of other business is so great that the majority leader often decides to let the recalcitrant senator prevail. In the final days before adjournment of Congress, when time was at a premium, Senator Howard Metzenbaum of Ohio would take his seat in the Senate chamber and insist on personally approving each bill or amendment before it was brought to the floor. His threat was to object to the proposal and to speak at length against it, thereby tying up the Senate and blocking action on any legislation. It was enormous leverage in the hands of one person, leading then majority leader Bob Dole to call Senator Metzenbaum the Commissioner.

Our system of checks and balances, and certainly the United States Senate, exists to protect the rights of minorities. The idea of one person standing firmly on principle, even if standing alone, is more than the plot of the movie *Mr. Smith Goes to Washington*, it is an American ideal. As Andrew Jackson said, "One man with courage makes a majority." But it is also true that in a democracy, the will of the people rules. If everyone insisted on blocking everything all the time, the result would be governmental paralysis—an inability of the democratic process to reach some sort of practical accommodation on matters the country needs to resolve.

The possibility of reaching practical accommodation on a given issue can turn, at least in part, on the way in which we relate religious faith to politics. If we believe that our political positions are implementations of God's will, then whatever stand we take becomes a matter of principle. Our political causes become religious crusades, and reasonable accommodation becomes difficult if not impossible to achieve. On the other hand, if we are less confident about our capacity to know and implement God's will, and if our faith brings modesty about ourselves and our politics, our effectiveness is more likely. I believe that such modesty is, or at least should be, Christianity's gift to American politics.

Christianity is a reality check about government, its laws and whatever role we have in making those laws. It is the antidote to our grandiosity about ourselves and about whatever political battle we might be fighting. To reflect on what we say we believe as Christians should bring us down to earth. Thinking back on my self-esteem, especially in those early years in the Senate, it is clear that I did not do a good enough job of reflecting on my own beliefs. But maybe it is never too late to start.

Christianity reminds us of the infinite distance between the people we are and the people God calls us to be. It reminds us of the infinite distance between God's commandments and any political philosophy or law or amendment to a law that we can devise. It evokes a humility that was clearly lacking in me and, I think, is often lacking in people who label their political ideas "Christian." It evokes humility because its standard is so much higher than anything we can embody in legislation, even if we act with the best of intentions and use our best efforts.

The standard is the Love Commandment, and there is never any excuse for my letting it drift out of my mind, no matter how focused I might be on my own causes. I certainly recited it enough times at the altar, especially in the early years of my ministry when it was written into the liturgy of the Episcopal Church. It should have been permanently engraved in my consciousness: "Hear what our Lord Jesus Christ saith: 'Thou shalt love the Lord thy God with all thy heart, and with all thy soul, and with all thy mind. This is the first and great commandment. And the second is like unto it: Thou shalt love thy neighbor as thyself. On these two commandments hang all the Law and the Prophets" (Book of Common Prayer).

That is the Summary of the Law, but it is not really a summary of a set of laws, since it preempts everything else, even the law God gave to Moses. The Gospels make this clear as Jesus repeatedly chooses to heal the sick even when doing so conflicts with legal demands to observe the sabbath. If the Love Commandment takes precedence over the law God gave Moses, it is even more certain that it takes precedence over any legislative program or political cause we can devise.

The error of the Christian Right is that in its attempt to codify the requirements of faith in a legislative program, it crowds out the demands of the Love Commandment. The effect is that law takes precedence over love, rather than the other way around. Conservatives want government to define when life begins as not at conception but at, in their new term, "inception," in the laboratory, without an embryo's being present in a potential mother. The government action they advocate would block early stage stem cell research, and it would criminalize scientists who are trying to find cures for diseases that cause untold human misery and death. For people who take seriously the claim of the Love Commandment on their lives, such legislation would block them from doing the healing work God calls them to do.

Government cannot take the position that each individual is a law unto himself, free to break the laws of the state and do whatever he pleases so long as he claims he is following his personal understanding of the Love Commandment. The masculine pronoun is convenient here because the two examples I will use to make the point involve men. The first is the famous case of Dr. Jack Kevorkian, the serial mercy-killing physician who believed he was acting in a loving way toward suffering patients by putting them out of their misery. In effect, the state said, "Whatever you think is loving, you cannot kill people." The second example was a case of sexual harassment. A man I knew admitted to a series of sexual relationships with women who worked under his supervision. He claimed that there was nothing wrong with his activities because he was giving pleasure, love and meaning to the lives of women who would be less happy for want of his attentions. I suspect he was rationalizing the satisfaction of his own sexual appetite, but his explanation was that he was giving love to others.

Like the harasser, it is possible, even likely, that we twist the commandment to love our neighbor into love of self. Even our best intentions toward others are mingled with the pursuit of our own interests. We want to do well by doing good. We want people to recognize us for our generosity. We want our name on a plaque or on a list of donors. We want a tax deduction for our charitable giving.

This is the real world in which government operates, the world of sinners and saints, and a lot of people who are some of each. So government suppresses our worst instincts—that is the role of criminal law—and it encourages our best instincts by the Peace Corps, the faith-based initiative and the charitable deduction in the tax code. And nearly all that government does in this real world of saints and sinners is earnestly debated by good people who disagree about where government should draw its lines. When exactly does life begin so that government should step in and protect it? If the government imprisons Dr. Kevorkian, must it keep a feeding tube in Terri Schiavo? Is the faith-based initiative merely helping religious groups do their jobs, or is it governmental intervention into religion? These are the kinds of questions we ask as government creates, evolves, re-creates and enforces its standards for society. The work of government calls for human judgment and compromise. It should be informed by the Love Commandment, but it is not the Love Commandment. Faith is not the same as politics.

Christians live within a system of law created by legislators doing the business of government, with all the compromises that entails. As the cliché puts it, politics is the art of the possible. Its method is give-and-take. Its values are the values of society, changing gradually as society changes. The Love Commandment can influence this system of law and the values it represents, but the system of law cannot encapsulate the Love Commandment, because the standard of love for Christians so greatly exceeds anything government can produce.

For Christians, the standard of love, and therefore the standard of human behavior, is the Cross. It is the Christ who emptied himself of equality with God, and gave himself up to suffering and death (Philippians 2:6–8). It is not the kind of love that expects something in return. It is the opposite of doing well by doing good. It is totally sacrificial. Because Christ is true man, as we are, it is the standard applicable to all of us. Because Christ is true God, as we are not, it is a standard we do not attain. Reinhold Niebuhr called it the "impossible possibility." It is relevant to our lives. It points us toward living beyond ourselves and for others. It leads some people to heroic acts: Mother Teresa in India, Medal of Honor winners who sacrifice themselves for their comrades. It leads most of us to occasional acts of generosity, even when we have nothing to gain. But for almost all of us, almost all the time, the words of the centurion to Jesus are appropriate: "Lord, I am not worthy that thou shouldest come under my roof: but speak the word only, and [thy] servant shall be healed" (Matthew 8:8, KJV).

So is the Love Commandment relevant to the world of practical politics? Yes, it is. It is always before us as the standard by which we measure everything we do. It is God's judgment against indifference to others and greed for ourselves. It reminds us of God's call to be faithful people, not only in our personal lives but in our politics. But does any political agenda we create warrant our claim that it is the embodiment of God's will? No, it does not. That goes for the Christian Right. That goes for the Christian Left.

A Quest for Certainty

The Love Commandment does not include detailed instructions on how to lead faithful lives. It leaves the implementing decisions to us, which, if we are conscientious people, creates a lot of uncertainty about whether we are truly doing God's will. Saint Paul told the Philippians to "[w]ork out your own salvation with fear and trembling; for it is God who is at work in you, enabling you both to will and to work for his good pleasure." We have to work out our own salvation; that is, we must find our own path in following our Lord, and that is a heavy responsibility. We proceed with fear and trembling, even as we know that God is at work in us.

It would be easier simply to follow instructions, to do as we are told. Then we might stray from the right path, but at least we would know if we were on it. Many of us would rather have less fear and trembling and more certainty in our lives. So a religion that tells us clearly the course we should follow provides a great deal of assurance and has a lot of appeal. Hence the popularity of conservative Christianity with its confidence that it comprehends God's will and can translate it into public policy.

I understand the appeal of that kind of clarity. It appeals to me. Some people's lives seem to progress in a straight line as they move purposefully from one year to another, confident that their every step will move them closer to their preordained destinations. They always knew they would be lawyers or doctors, so there they are. In my case, the course was zigzaggy, fitful and characterized by the kind of self-doubt Saint Paul described when he wrote to the Philippians. Was I doing what God wanted me to do, or was it only what I wanted to do? Along that zigzaggy path, I longed for clearer directions than I ever received.

Commenting on my college thesis about his colleague Reinhold Niebuhr, Professor John Bennett, of Union Theological Seminary, wrote that I demonstrated "a quest for certainty" that was characteristic of my generation. I am not sure about my generation, but I know about my own unsuccessful quest for certainty. It is the story of my life.

Politics is not in the Danforth genes. Until I came along, no member of my family had sought or held a political office, or shown much of an interest in elections or government. No doubt, my ancestors were good citizens who voted; certainly my parents did. But politics was almost never the fare at the family dinner table. It wasn't that my family was against politics; it was only that they didn't give it much attention. To date, at least, my five children have reverted to this family trait. Given the experience of campaigning for their dad, none of them has shown the slightest interest in pursuing my career.

Political ambition came upon me in a single moment. My parents had taken my brother Don and me for our first visit to Washington after we attended brother Bill's graduation from Princeton. Ten years old, sitting in the Senate Gallery, I had never seen anything as exciting as action on the Senate floor. What I wanted to be when I grew up was instantly clear to me. I wanted to be a United States senator.

I recall the first words my dad said as we filed out of the Senate Gallery: "What a bunch of windbags." But that was before I had a chance to express my own excitement or had breathed a word about my new ambition. As soon as they learned of my enthusiasm for politics, my parents were consistently supportive of me, and remained so for the rest of their days. That was the nature of my relationship with my parents. They expressed no expectation that I go into business or pursue any other particular course. I liked politics and that was good enough for them. It did not matter that it had never been one of their interests. Very often my mother said, "Back Jack." It had the ring of a campaign slogan, but its real meaning was that my parents were behind me in whatever I wanted to do. It was not exactly what Saint Paul had written to the Philippians, but it carried the same message of freedom and personal responsibility. I was to work out my own life, not with fear and trembling, but with enthusiasm.

My family was, and remains, the great blessing of my life. Even at ten years of age, I was ambitious, and what motivated me was a desire to make my family proud. I was never afraid of my parents the way some children are. My only fear was disappointing them. For their part, they always let me know that they loved me and were proud of me, even where pride was unmerited.

It was clear to my family and friends that I was going to be a politician—so clear to my high school classmates that they sometimes called me Senator. A natural way to go into politics was through the practice of law, so my objective, from sixth grade through junior year in college, was to go to law school, practice law and run for public office. Then, in the summer before my senior year in college, I changed my course toward ministry.

My religious upbringing was in the tradition of nineteenth-century Protestant liberalism, a school of thought that, at least in my family, did not carry with it any political implications. Protestant liberalism connoted an emphasis on the ethical teachings of Jesus and the perfectibility of humankind, with an accompanying de-emphasis of theology and the redemptive work of Christ.

My grandfather William H. Danforth was a great man, a charismatic leader before the word "charisma" became overused. A child of the nineteenth century, he was born in the Missouri boot heel in 1870, and moved to St. Louis, first for college, then to found Ralston Purina Company. He was colorful, usually dressed in his company's trademark checkerboard, and intent on inspiring people, especially young people, to live worthwhile lives. To that end, he founded summer camps for youths, and he wrote a book, *I Dare You!*, to promote his vision of the fourfold life. Again, his chosen symbol was the checker, the four squares of which stood for the physical, mental, social and religious aspects of life.

William Danforth coined a series of motivational slogans beginning with the words of his book title. They were:

I dare you to stand tall, think tall, smile tall, live tall.

I dare you to be your own self at your very best all the time.

I dare you to aspire nobly, adventure daringly, serve humbly.

Before his death, my grandfather claimed he had more than a million readers of *I Dare You!*, a book still in circulation. His summer camps, operated by the American Youth Foundation, which he founded, remain in operation. Even fifty years after his death, I hear from people who tell me that he changed their lives for the better.

I, too, read *I Dare You!* I, too, attended one of the summer camps: Miniwanca, in Michigan, where I was steeped in the four-fold way. And if William H. Danforth was an inspiration to countless young people, he was even more of an inspiration to his grandson, who saw him regularly and who received the added challenge to uphold the family's honor.

The slogan he reserved for our family, which he included in annual birthday letters, was "Cast no stigma on the Danforth escutcheon." Do nothing to damage the family name. Danforths have a special obligation to be our own selves at our very best all the time.

The problem was that I did not live up to my grandfather's high ideals, or in my own mind, to the pride my parents continually expressed in me. It was not that I was a terribly bad person, but I was not Mister Goody Good, especially in my first year or so in college, when the loosening of home-front restraints coincided with the availability of alcohol. During my late teens, I was a far cry from being my own self at my very best all the time, and the liberal religious training I had received as a child was not sufficient to provide much help.

I was a child of the church, baptized as an infant, educated in its Sunday school and confirmed. The parish of my childhood, as it is today, was St. Michael and St. George, which, at the time, was exceedingly low church and, itself, in the lineage of nineteenth-century Protestant liberalism. The message was consistent with my upbringing. It taught that the core of Christianity was to follow the teachings of Jesus and be a good person. But I was not being a good person. I quested, if not yet for certainty, at least for more substance in my faith. Then came the Department of Religion at Princeton.

I had not considered taking a college course in religion until a faculty adviser suggested that I fill a hole in my sophomore schedule with a course in Christian ethics taught by Paul Ramsey. Ramsey was a highly respected, conservative ethicist whose course included the subjects of sex and marriage and Christian teachings on just war. He was a compelling lecturer, delivering academic material in a southern accent with evangelical zeal. Speaking of sexuality, he said, "When some people say, 'I love you,' they mean 'I love me, and want you.'"

One course in the Princeton religion department led to another, and that led to my majoring in religion. I was reading Augustine, Aquinas and Kierkegaard. I was learning that Christianity consisted of much more than exhorting people to live good lives, an exhortation that had only limited impact on me. I was learning that Christianity had real substance, beyond my own feelings, beyond my willpower. It was a conversion experience, more of the mind than of the heart.

Princeton requires the writing of a senior thesis, and I chose to write about one of the great figures of the American church, Reinhold Niebuhr. My particular topic was his Christology, his understanding of Christ, but the importance of the project was that it forced me to read all of Niebuhr's books. That had an enormous effect on me, and on how I think about the relationship of Christianity to politics, even though my political views turned out to be significantly more conservative than Niebuhr's.

Niebuhr's own history included the disavowal of the Protestant liberalism of his younger years in favor of what he called Christian realism. His experience as an inner-city pastor during the Great Depression, followed by the rise of Nazism in Germany, shattered his early optimism that humankind could improve itself if only it willed itself to do so. This disavowal coincided with my own recognition that exhortations and willpower were not enough to transform me into the person my family and I expected me to be.

From Protestant liberalism through Niebuhrian realism, I then proceeded to the opposite end of the theological pole. It was a move that began with the writing of my Princeton thesis, which prompted Professor Bennett's comment about my "quest for certainty." Although impressed by Niebuhr's realism about the imperfectibility of humankind and the moral ambiguity of politics, I was critical of his understanding of Christ, thinking it lacking in theological content. To Niebuhr, Christ seemed less the Redeemer than the lens through which he saw human nature. I wrote, "While it is necessary for man to recognize the limitation of his knowledge of God, it is equally necessary to make definite statements about what he does know." Criticizing Niebuhr, I continued, "The Savior loses the element of mystery, which surrounds positive statements about an actuality, and he becomes the object of an intellectual exercise, which has at its end statements about the meaning of life and not a faith in the Redemption of the world."

My shift in emphasis from the moral implications of Christianity to its theological content continued after I graduated from Princeton. Inspired by Paul's letter to the Romans, Martin Luther's defense of justification by faith alone and the heavily Christocentric writings of Karl Barth, I became convinced that humankind is justified by the death and resurrection of Christ, not only without works, but despite bad works. Here was the answer to my earlier guilt about not being my best self. Why feel responsible, much less guilty, if Christ takes care of everything? A more balanced and, I think, faithful view is that the free gift of God in Christ increases, not lessens, our responsibility to live as good people.

Fascinated as I was by my Princeton studies in religion, I gave no thought to divinity school and possible ordination until the summer of 1957, the summer between my junior and senior years at college. There was no doubt I was going to law school after graduation—no doubt in my mind and no doubt in the mind of my bride to be, Sally Dobson.

Today, looking back from the standpoint of a parent, Sally and I were too young and immature to get married. She turned twenty that July, and my twenty-first birthday was two days before our wedding in September. But we were passionately in love and did not want to wait to get married, so with the approval of our parents and of the university, I became what was a rarity at then all-male Princeton: a married undergraduate. Sally and I would not have married at that early age over the objection of our parents, and under university rules at the time, I could not have married and remained an undergraduate without Princeton's consent. Immature as we were, we were given the freedom to create our own destiny.

Marriage at a young age can be a disaster, but when it works, it really works; and in our case, after forty-nine years, I can say it really worked. As people say, in marriage there are bumps along the way, but we had only one big bump and it was a monster. It happened in the living room of her parents' home in St. Louis two months before the ceremony when, with no warning, I told Sally I was going to seminary.

The granddaughter of a Presbyterian minister, who had seen in her family what it means to be a clergy wife and a clergy family, Sally wanted none of it. It would mean a dramatic change in the life she thought she was going to lead, with my doing something she thought I was not suited to do and her being married not just to me but to a parish church. For my part, I trusted that God was leading me in this direction, either to serve in the parish ministry or to teach, but I had heard no clear call to the ministry. I supposed rather than knew that this was God's will for me.

At Yale Divinity School, my quest for certainty took a new turn, toward a longing for an authoritative Church. In a first-year theology class, each student was required to select a part of the Apostles' Creed and write a paper on it. I chose to write on the Church, or at least on what I thought should be a doctrine of the Church. It was a ridiculous topic to pick in a predominantly Protestant divinity school, where little deference was paid to ecclesiastical hierarchies, and the paper received a well-deserved mediocre grade. But my argument did succeed in expressing the state of my mind at the time. I thought there was such a thing as God's truth, which could be expressed in doctrine, and the institutional Church was the truth's custodian. Rather than relying on the Bible as the repository of the faith or attempting to understand the great theologians, I wanted someone "up there" to tell me what to believe.

At about that time, I had a conversation with my father in which he expressed dismay about the divided state of Christianity. He thought there should be a major ecumenical effort to bring the denominations together. As a know-it-all divinity student, I immediately belittled his opinion. I told him that such an ecumenical effort would not work because, in my view, all denominations did not equally share the truth.

A Quest for Certainty

My quest for theological certainty was accompanied by growing vocational uncertainty, and by the end of my first year at Yale Divinity School, it was clear to me that I had made a mistake. I had neither the temperament to be a good parish minister nor the abstract kind of mind to be a good teacher of religion. But the clarity of the decision came after months of turmoil and the unhappiest time of my life. Did God want me to stay the course? Did God want me to leave divinity school? I sought counsel from a Yale professor who had a reputation for giving good spiritual guidance to students. I knocked on his door and entered his office, but he barely raised his eyes from his desk. He never invited me to sit down. I blurted out my concern, and he brusquely said that God was not forcing me to do something I did not want to do. That was it. I was dismissed. No direction seemed to come from God. No interest came from the divinity school. No certainty came from any source. Finally, in the summer after my first year as a seminarian, I made my own decision. A life in the ministry did not seem right to me. On the basis of feeling, I made a change of course that brought tremendous relief. But my decision came too late in the year to switch academic direction, so I continued my second year at the divinity school and gained acceptance to Yale Law School for the following year.

Because it seemed a waste to complete two thirds of my seminary work without earning a degree, I asked Liston Pope, the dean of Yale Divinity School, if I could spread my final two semesters of theological education over the three years of law school so I could receive both degrees at the same time. He replied that there was a rule against spreading one year's work over more than two years, but said he would think it over and get back to me. A week later, Dean Pope phoned to say he was waiving the rule and giving his permission. In his words, "Being a minister and a lawyer is an interesting combination. It's like being a striptease saint."

Yale Law School is one of the best places I know—an assemblage of extraordinary minds and idealistic personalities who are intensely interested in the law and the policy behind it. Course work consisted of reading cases in preparation for classes where professors singled out students for Socratic questioning about changing hypothetical fact patterns. Participating in classes and interacting with other students outside the classroom was an intellectual workout that contrasted with what I thought to be the sluggishness of theological education. My enjoyable law school experience confirmed my decision that my future should be in law and politics. But the question of what to do with a degree from the divinity school remained open. Yet more uncertainty about my future rekindled my longing for the authoritative voice of the Church. I did not want to take responsibility for my own life. I wanted someone else to tell me what to do.

A principal role of the bishop of a diocese is to be the pastor to his clergy and seminarians. The bishop of Missouri in those years, George L. Cadigan, was the most pastoral clergyperson I have ever known. He was kind, gentle and patient, thoughtfully counseling his seminarians from the deep reserves of his own spirituality. His approach resembled that of my parents during my childhood. He was not directive, nor inclined to tell me what he wanted me to do, encouraging me to follow the course that seemed best to me.

But I wanted his direction on the important decision before me: Should I be ordained to the priesthood of the Episcopal Church? My own conviction was that the priesthood is a vocation in which a clear call from God was a condition of being ordained. I had heard no such call. Instead of a clear conviction, I was ambivalent. So my hope was that my bishop would instruct me about what to do. If Bishop Cadigan would just tell me, it would take responsibility out of my own hands. My main concern was that my own decision for ordination might be selfish. It might be satisfying a desire for status. After all, as an ordained lawyer and politician, I would have the status of a priest without the daily responsibilities of the priesthood.

Law school was demanding, and it left little time for work at the divinity school, where I took one course each semester. For courses, I selected seminars that met once a week. I regularly cut those meetings. I wrote papers in lieu of taking exams, and chose exceedingly narrow topics for my papers to minimize the reading I would have to do. I attended summer school at Union Theological Seminary to gain some credits, but for the most part, I got through my third year of divinity school with very little effort. The ease with which I skated through that final year and the light load I knew I would carry should I be ordained raised questions in my mind about my authenticity as a potential priest.

During my law school years, I had occasional and always inconclusive meetings with Bishop Cadigan about my future. No decision was made until the Christmas holiday of my final year in law school. Bishop Cadigan was to hold some sort of meeting at Thompson House, an Episcopal retreat house in St. Louis County, and he asked me to see him after the meeting. For some time we went back and forth on the ordination question; the bishop would ask what I wanted to do, and I would respond, "What do you want me to do, Bishop?" It was clear that he would not budge from his nondirective stance. Finally, he asked one more time, "What do you want to do, Jack?" Having run out of further equivocation, I responded, "I think I should be ordained." To that he replied, "I want you to be ordained."

Not long after that meeting with Bishop Cadigan, the most well-known dual-vocation priest in America appeared as a guest speaker at an evening program at Christ Church, New Haven. William Pollard was a nuclear physicist who had been ordained, and was practicing both vocations in Tennessee. He was very highly regarded in the Episcopal Church and beyond. At the conclusion of the program, I went to the front of the church, told him of my future intentions, and asked if I could meet with him before he left town. I was anxious to get whatever advice he had to offer on how to combine the priesthood with another profession. Pollard did not know me, and he tried to brush me off, saying that he was leaving New Haven the next morning. I virtually begged him to meet with me before his scheduled departure, even if it was very early in the morning. He relented, and invited me to join him for breakfast at the Yale Faculty Club.

It was not a long meeting, but Pollard's advice was clear and very important. He said that it is difficult to do two jobs well, and that my tendency would be to let the ministry slide as my life became preempted by the practice of law. To offset this tendency in his own life, he had established two rules, which gave his ministry some discipline and which he commended to me. First, he said it was important to be officially connected to a parish church, with some sort of title, and to be included on the list of parish clergy. Second, he said it was important to have some fixed responsibility within the congregation, even if it is a small one. An example would be responsibility for a group within the congregation, or for the pastoral care of some shut-ins.

Until my sixty-fifth birthday, when I began being content to sit in a pew beside my wife, I followed Pollard's advice. For example, throughout my Senate years, I was listed as Honorary Associate in the Sunday bulletins of St. Alban's Church, and I had two regular responsibilities: I celebrated the Eucharist at the 7:30 A.M. Tuesday service, and I took Communion to two or three shut-ins approximately every five weeks.

For the first three years after graduating from Yale, I practiced law at Davis Polk and served as assistant rector at the Church of the Epiphany in New York City. The rector at Epiphany was a salty and wonderful character named Hugh McCandless, who took a special interest in including a variety of outlying clergy like me in the work of the parish. He assigned me to hospital chaplaincy work under the supervision of the Reverend Carleton Sweetser, then the chaplain at four East Side hospitals.

My Sunday mornings began in the small chapel of Memorial Hospital, usually with only three people present. Either Carleton or I celebrated the Eucharist, the third person being a nurse who regularly attended. Memorial is a cancer hospital, and the intimate experience of services in that setting was extraordinarily spiritual. After the celebration, Carleton and I divided the responsibility of taking the sacrament to patients in their rooms—Carleton to those in Memorial Hospital, while I went to New York Hospital across the street. Many of the patients I saw, even in New York Hospital, suffered from cancer. Many were close to death. Some had undergone radical surgery to remove limbs. A few were missing both legs. I witnessed in these patients the range of human response, from the heights of great faith to the depths of despair. Seeing these people, even for short visits, was such a moving experience that, for a brief time, I considered reversing course yet again, and leaving the law for the hospital chaplaincy. It was another instance of uncertainty, a vague sense that God might be tugging me in a different direction, but there was no clear indication that this was a calling. Again I decided that the original course of law and politics better suited my personality.

Even while following William Pollard's advice of being connected with a parish church and undertaking at least a modicum of fixed responsibilities, I always realized that I was a fifth wheel among the parish clergy. Where they devoted perhaps fifty or sixty hours a week to their ministries, I devoted perhaps one or two hours. Where they had to be available to their parishioners, often at the expense of their families, I could let things slide for as long as I wanted, knowing that someone else would do my work. During election years when I was in the Senate, I could be away from St. Alban's weeks at a time, and the parish would be none the worse for my absence.

As a group, the clergy I have known have been outstanding individuals. They have been caring pastors with genuine empathy for their people. Some of them have been gifted preachers and teachers. Some have had remarkable spiritual insight. All have been dedicated to their calling. All have been hardworking. Nearly all have had careers far less remunerative than those of their parishioners. I cannot overstate my admiration for the parish clergy and my belief in the importance of their vocations.

Compared to them, I could come and go as I pleased. While they were laboring in their churches, I was going to the Capitol. While they were visiting the sick, I was speaking in the Senate. While they were comforting the brokenhearted, I was meeting with heads of state. While they were struggling to support their families, I was enjoying an income many times theirs.

In the 1970s, I had the privilege of meeting Henri Nouwen, a Dutch Catholic priest who taught at Yale Divinity School. A person of great spiritual depth, Nouwen had written *The Wounded*

Healer, a little book that was immensely popular with the clergy. In the book, Nouwen described the loneliness of the parish ministry, its clergy left behind in the neighborhoods of their churches while parishioners were doing society's real work, a clergy marginalized by the laity when important decisions were being made. For Nouwen, this loneliness was a strength, enabling a wounded clergy to empathize with the injured and alienated people of a broken world, and through that empathy, to bring healing to others.

Nouwen's premise that the work of the Church is the ministry of reconciliation, healing our brokenness with God and with each other, had great appeal to me. It continues to be the way I understand the Church's mission in the world, and the way I think Christians should relate to politics. God calls us to be the healing Church. The ordained clergy working in the parish is at the center of our healing ministry. I was impressed by Nouwen's insight that the capacity of the clergy to empathize with human suffering, drawn from its own suffering, was a source of the ministry of healing. Nouwen's emphasis was not on what individual clergy said or did. It was not on brilliant preaching or effective pastoral care. Instead, he emphasized what the clergy was by its very nature. It was the wounded healer.

But Nouwen's description of the ministry did not describe me. I had not been left behind in the parish. I wasn't holding the hands of grieving widows. I wasn't struggling to educate my children. I was pontificating on the great issues of the day in the comfort of a privileged lifestyle. Among the clergy, whom I respect so much, I was a dilettante.

Should I have chosen ordination when I met with Bishop Cadigan that day at Thompson House? I have asked that question of myself for more than four decades, sometimes yielding one answer, sometimes the other. As usual, certainty eludes me. I think, now, that the answer is yes, but I cannot justify the answer by any specific contribution I have made to the ministry, only by the symbolism of being an ordained person who does secular work. With full knowledge that my explanation may be a rationalization for an inadequate ministry, I do think that the symbolism of an ordained lawyer/politician is significant.

It has to do with the Incarnation, that is, as John's Gospel states it, "The Word became flesh and dwelt among us." The holy and transcendent God did not choose to remain apart from us, even when we had fallen from God, but condescended to be with us in the flesh. So the Church of the Incarnate God, the body of Christ, is in the world. It does not isolate itself. It goes where the people are. In that sense, Christianity is a worldly religion. It is in the world and not of it. At least in my mind, the combination of the ordained ministry with other occupations symbolizes the presence of the Church in the world.

Perhaps this is a good point from which to offer a short summary of where I am theologically, acknowledging that my days of serious theological study are in the distant past.

Participants in the daily prayers of the Episcopal Church recite the Apostles' Creed. At the Eucharist, believers join in the Nicene Creed. In each service, the creed begins with the words "I (or we) believe," and proceeds with ancient statements of the Christian faith. When I say those words, I mean what I say. The Nicene Creed confesses belief in one God who is the "maker . . . of all that is, seen and unseen." It goes on to state the belief in Jesus Christ, whom it describes as "true God from true God" and "of one Being with the Father." It says that this "one Lord, Jesus Christ . . . became incarnate from the Virgin Mary, and was made man," that he was crucified, that he died, that "on the third day he rose again," that he "ascended into heaven," that "he will come again in glory" and that "his kingdom will have no end." The Nicene Creed proceeds to state belief in the Holy Spirit, in "one holy catholic and apostolic church," in "one baptism," in "the resurrection of the dead, and the life of the world to come."

That is what I believe, and in so believing, I am one with Christians who have recited the same words for something like seventeen hundred years. I am in no way unconventional in my Christian faith. What reading I have done by writers who have attempted to "reimagine" Christianity, or restate it in terms thought to be more acceptable to the modern age, has not impressed me. Rather, it has often seemed a watering down of the faith to the point of becoming something not worth believing. Saint Paul wrote the Corinthians that "if Christ has not been raised, our preaching is in vain and your faith is in vain." The death and resurrection of Christ is the heart of the Christian faith. Preaching Jesus as merely a good person who is an example of good living falls short of preaching the Gospel.

Recently, there has been a well-publicized debate about the compatibility of religion and science. In my mind, there is no incompatibility unless science breaches basic rules of ethics, for example, by attempting to create human beings through reproductive cloning, an idea universally rejected by ethicists. I understand the Genesis account of creation as a statement of faith and not as a scientific document, so I do not share the determination of creationists to include their beliefs in school curricula. I believe that God is the creator of all things, and that God is actively involved in our lives and in history, which would put me in line with the intelligent design advocates, except that I think it is a religious concept that should not be taught in public schools.

While I am a believing Christian, I acknowledge the distance between God's reality and our perception of that reality. I do not believe that any faith, including my own, monopolizes human understanding of God. I believe that God created and embraces all humankind, and that religious bigotry against anyone is more than uncivilized, it is in opposition to Christianity.

If my quest for certainty, commented on by Professor Bennett, found refuge in a conventional understanding of Christian theology, it was far from satisfied by the rapidly changing course of my life. Until well into my final year of law school, Sally and I intended on graduation to return to our hometown of St. Louis. Then, on a whim, I accepted an offer from a New York law firm, now known as Davis Polk & Wardwell, where I was a member of the Tax Department. Three years later, we changed course again and returned to St. Louis, where I joined what is now Bryan Cave, a firm where I have since spent the nonpublic periods of my career.

By the spring of 1968, Sally and I had three daughters, and Sally was expecting again. I had completed a seven-week criminal trial, where I was the court-appointed counsel for one of several defendants, and had decided to make my first run for public office. So, at age thirty-one, I filed as a Republican candidate for Missouri attorney general, against an incumbent and in a state that hadn't elected a Republican to any statewide office in more than two decades. I was politically unknown, and an extreme long shot, and I assured Sally I had no chance of being elected.

Four weeks before the election, Sally delivered our fourth daughter, Jody. Then, to the astonishment of nearly everyone, I won.

St. Louis Republicans had scheduled a victory party at the Khorassan Room of the Chase Park Plaza, but, of course, they didn't mean it. It was the quadrennial ritual of renting and decorating a ballroom, getting together for food and drinks, receiving the expected bad news and going home. When the results came in and I had won, they were beside themselves with joy, shouting and whistling, pounding me on the back. Then I saw, sitting on the edge of the stage, her head down with sorrow, the love of my life, literally floored by shock at the victory, disappointment that we would leave St. Louis, and postpartum blues. Winning elections had been my childhood dream, but sometimes dreams are happier than reality.

The next night, we were at my parents' farm outside Washington, Missouri, talking about this new reality. The attorney general was required by law to live in Jefferson City, a place we learned to enjoy greatly, but at the time seemed the other end of the world from St. Louis. What had we gotten into? Talking it out, we decided that for six months I would live in a motel. Then at the end of the school year, Sally and the children would follow me to Jefferson City, where we would stay for three years, returning to St. Louis for the beginning of the school year before the end of my term. That, we decided, would be my only time as an elected officeholder. Twenty-six years later, after two terms as attorney general, three terms in the Senate, and a fifth child, a son, I retired from elective office.

During those twenty-six years, many people asked me to explain the relationship between my ministry and my public service. I always told them that the people of Missouri had hired me to be their attorney general or their senator. They did not hire me to be their pastor. Missouri is a state of five and a half million people, slightly less than one half of 1 percent of whom are Episcopalians. They are members of every conceivable religious denomination or have no religion at all. My job was to serve all these millions of people, so it would have been inappropriate to foist my religion on them. It would have been worse than inappropriate: It would have been divisive and wrong. Because the task of government is to hold together in one country a diverse public, my interjection of religion into politics would have been a profound disservice to my state and my country. It would have sown division where there should be unity.

While disclaiming the role of pastor, I always told my constituents that in electing someone to public office, they were electing a whole person, with all of the background and values that constitute a person. A public official is not a disembodied collection of policy positions, but a unique human being with all that entails. In my case, I was the totality of a lifetime. I was a Christian and I was an Episcopal priest, not just on Sundays, not just when I was in church, but every minute of every day, wherever I was. I brought the totality of myself to public office. When I entered the Senate, I did not check my religion at the door.

There is a difference between being a Christian in politics and having a Christian agenda for politics. There were times when I believed that on a particular issue, I was doing God's will. My attempts to address the hunger crises in Cambodia and Africa were times of such belief, but such times were very rare. For the overwhelming majority of my time in public life, I had no certainty that my side was God's side.

Throughout my years in the Senate, I voted against the death penalty. That position was consistent with what I thought of as religious values, but I did not justify it on religious grounds. My argument was that government should not take lives unless it was necessary to save lives, and since the death penalty did not statistically reduce crime, the test of saving lives had not been met. I certainly did not claim that my position was God's position and that, therefore, the majority of Missourians who supported the death penalty were wrong. Many of them were at least as religious as I.

If, in the divine plan, there were sure answers to questions of public policy, God seldom gave them to me. If God gave the answers to anyone, a lot must have been lost in translation, for on the "religious issues"—abortion, stem cell research, public display of religion and the like—people who worship God are on opposing sides. If there is a Christian agenda for politics, what should it be? I, for one, cannot be certain.

Then one might ask, what does faith bring to politics if not an agenda? For me, it brings a struggle to do God's will that always falls short of the goal. It leavens the competing self-interests of politics with the yeast of the Love Commandment, but it seldom fulfills the Love Commandment. It makes us better participants in politics, but not the custodians of God's politics.

Most of all, faith brings recognition that our quest never leads us to certainty. We are always uncertain, always in doubt that our way is God's way. That self-doubt makes it possible to be reconciled to one another. It is a faith that makes the reconciling work of politics possible.

A LOOK AT THE WEDGE ISSUES

*H*aving struggled with my "quest for certainty," I understand the quest of many people for certainty about God's purpose for us. My daily prayer is shared by many Christians: "Grant O heavenly Father that I may know and do your will." We want to live in accordance with the will of God, so we want to know what that will is, with as much clarity as we can have.

Not long ago, a friend who is a Christian asked my counsel about a career decision. Should he remain in his present job, or should he accept an offer to go elsewhere? It was a turning point in his life, and a very difficult choice. I offered him assurance rather than career advice. I assured him that he would make the right decision because he wanted to make the right decision. I told him that because he was prayerfully opening himself to do God's will, he would do God's will, whatever path he chose. It was *counsel in line with my own experience. I believe that God was guiding me along my own career path without ordering me around. I was working out my own salvation with fear and trembling while God was at work in me. God was not relieving me of my own responsibility by making my decisions for me. That would have been too easy. Rather, God was working in me as I made my choices, and using those choices for his good pleasure. That, I believe, is how God works in us as we engage in politics; God guides us without ordering us around. God calls us to be faithful without handing us a political agenda.*

At least that's how I see faith and politics, but it is not how everyone sees faith and politics. Christian conservatives believe that God's will can be reduced to a political program, and that they have done so. In their minds, there is indeed a Christian agenda for America, and in recent years, they have succeeded in pressing it upon the Republican Party. It is an agenda comprised of wedge issues, which, when hammered relentlessly in political forums, divide the American people. So let us now examine those wedge issues, and ask ourselves whether they deserve the constant hammering or whether it would be better to try to hold the country together.

PUBLIC RELIGION

I go to the front of the church, where the priest makes a cross on my forehead with ashes made from last year's palms. It looks like a black smudge. After the service, I head for the door, the sunlight, the events of the day ahead. A question enters my mind, but not for long: with or without the smudge? Should I spend the rest of the day showing to the world that I am a Christian who went to church on the first day of Lent, or should I remove the smudge and blend in with everyone else?

No sooner am I out the door than I have whipped a handkerchief from my pants pocket and removed the smudge from my forehead. I check the vanity mirror on my car's sun visor to see if I got it all. I assure myself that I have put into practice the day's

Gospel reading: "... whenever you fast, do not look dismal, like the hypocrites, for they disfigure their faces so as to show others that they are fasting ... but when you fast, put oil on your head and wash your face ..." (Matthew 6:16–17).

But the truth is that removing the smudge from my forehead has nothing to do with the passage from Matthew. There is a different, and perhaps shameful, reason for what I have done. I am embarrassed to show the world that I have been to church. I want to blend in like everyone else.

Religion does and should make us uncomfortable. We know that we are not the people God created us to be, and that we should strive to be better than we are. Attending to that discomfort is the purpose of penitential times of the year. As the priest says when imposing ashes: "Remember that you are dust, and to dust you shall return." But that is a different kind of discomfort, a private recognition of who we are and what we should be. What bothers me as I exit the church on Ash Wednesday is something else—not private recognition that I am a sinner, but public embarrassment, undue self-consciousness about how my public practice of religion might appear to others.

It's like my embarrassment at grace before meals. We say grace at our family dinner table when we are alone and when we have guests. In our own home, the acknowledgment of God's blessing seems natural. What embarrasses me, to the point of not doing it unless pressed, is the offering of grace in public restaurants and dining rooms.

This feeling of embarrassment is wrong, and I'm sorry I have it. In Matthew 10:32–33, Jesus plainly says, "Everyone therefore who acknowledges me before others, I also will acknowledge before my Father in heaven; but whoever denies me before others, I also will deny before my Father in heaven." But knowing that the feeling is wrong doesn't make it go away.

The Noonday Club, appropriately named for the time of day when it does most of its business, is located on the top floor of the Metropolitan Square building in St. Louis, where my law firm, Bryan Cave, occupies eight floors. With commanding views of the Arch and the Mississippi River, it is the standard luncheon venue for lawyers, many of whom are from Bryan Cave, and it is a convenient place for businesspeople to meet. On a given day, I know perhaps half of the several scores of people in the spacious, sunny dining room. Frequently, I invite guests to have lunch with me, many of whom are clergy, most of whom are wearing clerical collars. Always, I suppose that my guest expects someone to say a blessing, and, conscious that I am surrounded by colleagues from the law firm and other acquaintances, I know that I don't want to be the one to do it. I ask my guest to offer thanks, and bow my head, imagining that all action in the restaurant has come to a halt, that food service has ceased, that every eye is focused on our table. Silently, telepathically, I plead with my guest, "Please keep it short." When the prayer ends, I exhale, take a sip of water, glance around the room to see who may have been watching and gather myself for the meal ahead.

I once confided my distress at giving restaurant blessings to my bishop, Hays Rockwell. He suggested that, if pressed, I should bow my head and say the shortest grace he knew, *Benedictus benedictat*, which means "May the Blessed One give blessing." He wrote this out on the back of his business card, which I have since carried in my wallet.

I suppose most people do not share my self-consciousness about open displays of religion. They wear religious symbols as jewelry. They retain ashes throughout Ash Wednesday. I am moved by the sight of people holding hands in a restaurant and quietly offering thanks for their meal. I wish I were less reticent, more open, more like them. I hope I am in the minority, but I am sure I am not alone in wanting not to stand out, wanting to blend in with everyone else. I think that accounts for people, especially first-time visitors, who prefer to sit in the back of churches, afraid to be noticed doing something wrong or to seem different and out of place.

In many churches, congregants "exchange the peace" during the service, greeting one another with handshakes or embraces. Some people are too self-conscious to feel comfortable doing that.

Years ago, I served as a supply priest in a parish in St. Louis County. When I arrived at the church about twenty minutes before the 8:00 A.M. service, I was immediately told by the person greeting me, "We don't exchange the peace here." Maybe ten minutes later, another parishioner came into the room where I was vesting to tell me, "We don't exchange the peace here." Then, just as I was about to begin the service, an usher said, "We don't exchange the peace here." It was clear that not exchanging the peace was more than an idiosyncrasy of that parish; it was a matter of overriding concern to the members that they be spared the self-conscious act of greeting one another.

The practice of religion is more than individual prayer, it is a communal act, a coming together of the people of God to worship God. Its work is to break down the barriers that separate us and bring us together. But for some of us, public displays of religion can make us feel self-conscious and alienated from other people. If these feelings are present even among Christians worshipping in the same parish church, if they affect even a member of the clergy anxious to remove a smudge from his face, they must be common when religious minorities find themselves participating in the religion of the majority.

From fifth grade through high school, I attended St. Louis Country Day School, a private, nonsectarian school for boys. The students represented a variety of religious traditions, and a number of them were Jewish. Several times a week, we attended a school assembly which, while called chapel, consisted mainly of remarks by the headmaster, announcements and sometimes outside speakers. I don't remember any religious content to these chapel meetings, except that at each meeting, the boys stood and sang a hymn. A standard hymn was "Holy, Holy, Holy." It did not bother me at all; indeed, the thought did not enter my mind that Jewish kids, with all the peer pressure of their schoolmates, and under the eyes of their teachers, were singing "Holy, Holy, Holy, merciful and mighty, God in three persons, blessed Trinity."

At least as a schoolboy, I was young and ignorant, with no role in the choice of hymns that were sung in my school. Many years later, I could no longer plead youth or ignorance when I committed an unimaginable act of insensitivity in the presence of thousands of onlookers. It was a June day in the 1970s, and the occasion was a Yale University commencement ceremony, truly one of the most splendid spectacles in American higher education. Yale does many things very well, but in my experience, it is without parallel in the grandeur and taste with which it conducts its commencements. Led by a university band, a long academic procession proceeds through the campus, diagonally to the center of the New Haven Green, through the main gate into the historic center of the university, the Old Campus. This expansive quadrangle is packed with proud parents, and the seats in front of the canopied stage slowly fill with black-robed students together with faculty, splendidly arrayed in colorful academic regalia. All the while, the band plays stirring marches. One can almost feel the hearts of the parents swelling with pride.

By the standards of other universities, the ceremony is very brief, lasting about an hour. There is no commencement speech, and diplomas are awarded later, at the residential colleges and graduate and professional schools. As if to underscore the brightness of the event, the weather at nearly every Yale commencement I have attended has been magnificently sunny.

For six years, I served on the Yale Corporation, the university's governing board, which accounted for my presence at a number of commencements in addition to my own and those of two daughters. On the day of my unimaginable act, it was my task to pronounce the blessing at the conclusion of the ceremony. For reasons I have long since neither understood nor excused, I read a blessing that invoked the name of God, "Father, Son and Holy Spirit," just as though I had said it in church. This was no accident, no temporary lapse of judgment. On the plane to New Haven the previous day, I had consciously picked the blessing out of a booklet. My fault, of course, was that many graduates, their families and their guests were not Christians. They were present to enjoy one of the proudest hours of their lives, and I had imposed my own religious observance on them. I am grateful that the university chaplain, William Sloane Coffin, took me to task immediately after the ceremony. The lesson has remained with me ever since that day. In public displays of religion, it is worth taking great care not to exclude those who do not share one's beliefs.

The most hawkish defenders of the separation of church and state see the establishment of religion even in such minimal religious references as the phrases "In God We Trust" on coins and "under God" in the Pledge of Allegiance. My own opinion is that this kind of usage is so routine and insubstantial that it could offend virtually no one, much less rise to the level of the establishment of religion. But if inoffensiveness is the test, it is the same as saying that public religion would be acceptable as long as it is innocuous.

What is or is not the establishment of religion within the meaning of the Constitution is a legal issue I will leave to the courts and to constitutional scholars. For present purposes, I am less interested in the state of the law than in the state of public religion, that is, the way in which religion is used in public settings, whether or not the sponsor of the public religion is government. In this connection, the political banquet warrants special attention.

Recently, I have noticed a revolutionary and welcome change in the design of political banquets, although the basic opening format of National Anthem, Pledge of Allegiance and prayer remains the same. The change is the demise of the head table (or tables) in favor of the dispersal of honored guests throughout the gym or ballroom.

The head table was the universal standard throughout my political career, and its decline in popularity tells me I was born a generation too soon. Always, the table was elevated on a stage or riser so its guests would be clearly visible to everyone in the crowd for every minute of the program. The principal speaker, say the senator or governor, invariably sat at the most honored position, at the center of the head table, immediately to the left or right of the rostrum. If you were the principal speaker, that meant that you had only one dinner companion, the person on the side other than the rostrum. This created an obvious vulnerability. If the one companion, often the master of ceremonies, was otherwise engaged in making notes or talking to someone else, you would find yourself not only very visible, but also the only person in the room with no one talking to you.

I think it was at an annual Lincoln Day dinner in Cape Girardeau, an event attended by nearly a thousand Republicans, where I learned a lesson: never accept the well-intentioned and very polite invitation to be the first person through the food line.

The Cape Girardeau Lincoln Day dinner takes place in a very large, terrazzo-floored, gymlike auditorium. To the right of the high, elevated head table is a stage where a skit about the life of Abraham Lincoln is performed later in the program. To the left is the quite extensive food line.

As a young politician and featured speaker, I accepted the invitation to be the first in line, filled my plate with fried chicken, string beans with bacon, potato salad and baked beans, and proceeded to the head table. I sat down and waited for what I assumed would be a few seconds for someone to join me. A minute passed, then another, then another. Then five minutes. Then I noticed that the other head table guests, all local officeholders or aspirants, were nowhere near joining me. They were working the food line, shaking every hand in the auditorium. Far from being first in line, they would be last.

Being conspicuously alone in the world is not a desired image for someone in politics. It is the opposite of the bandwagon effect that leads people to believe that your candidacy is being carried forward on a wave of popularity. Now you are all alone in a world of many hundreds of Republicans.

What to do? Is it better to eat by myself in front of all those people or to stare, smile, nod at them across the vast auditorium?

Each alternative is equally unappealing. The one certainty was my resolve never to be first in line if I was to sit at a head table.

Thinking about it, the idea of a head table was unnatural, but it did serve a political purpose: making politicians visible to their supporters. If the head table has been abandoned, the format of political dinners has not, for the format serves an even more important end than visibility. It creates the notion that politicians are both patriotic and religious.

Political banquets always begin with the singing of the National Anthem, followed by the Pledge of Allegiance, followed by the invocation. They almost always conclude with a benediction. Usually, but not necessarily, the invocation and the benediction are offered by clergy of different faiths. In the mind of a politician, dispensing with the National Anthem, or the Pledge or the invocation would be considered an unnecessary risk, possibly inviting supporters to have doubts about the candidate's patriotism or faith.

Since most nonprofit organizations, say the American Cancer Society or the community hospital, do not follow this set format of National Anthem, Pledge and prayer, one might ask what is different about political banquets. I doubt that the answer lies in a special degree of patriotism and religious devotion in politicians, and suspect that it has more to do with politicians' concern for maintaining appearances.

Of the thousands of prayers I have heard offered at political events, most have been nonsectarian and have consisted of all-purpose references to God. Some, offered by Christian clergy, have made reference to the Trinity, and have struck me as being insensitive to non-Christians in the audience, just as my prayer at the Yale commencement must have struck its hearers as insensitive.

Now consider the astute politician who invites two, or even better, three clergy to participate in the festivities, each representing a different faith. Should each pray in accordance with his or her own tradition, or should each offer a redundant, inoffensive, all-purpose prayer? In my experience, the majority of clergy taking part in such events opts for prayers that will satisfy almost everyone, even if the reason behind their selection is to convince the audience that the candidate is respectful of various faiths.

I have singled out political banquets because they are such striking examples of the public display of religion for an ulterior purpose, not so much to invoke the blessing of God, but to create the appearance of doing so. To serve such an end, prayer need not have much content. Beyond the world of politics, the general rule of innocuousness holds. Prayers at public events, political or not, are designed to be inoffensive and bland. They do acknowledge God, but in a de minimis way. If we heard such prayers in church, we would feel that we, as well as God, had been shortchanged. I have heard people say about such prayers, "What harm do they do?" Probably little, if any. The reverse of the question is equally apt. What good do they do? Same answer.

While the standard for public prayer is that it be innocuous, that is not the standard most religious people would apply to their own spiritual lives. Going through the formality of religion for the sake of appearances is exactly what Jesus criticized the Pharisees for doing. Christians who customarily pray in the name of Jesus and through Jesus would not consider the conscious omission of any reference to their Lord as doing justice to the demands of their faith.

So it is surprising that all-purpose public religion has generated such fervent support, especially from conservative Christians.

Recent controversies about the display of the Ten Commandments in courthouses in Alabama and Kentucky and on the state capitol grounds in Texas have inspired organized prayer meetings on courthouse steps, with the assembled faithful asking divine help and judicial wisdom that God not be taken out of our nation's life.

But the public display of religion is not God. We do not put God in our nation's life by placing the Ten Commandments in courthouses, nor do we evict God by removing the Ten Commandments from public property. God is not portable. Bland prayers, offered as noncontroversial formalities after the National Anthem and the Pledge of Allegiance do little to honor God.

I have heard people assert that public religion has a positive influence on behavior. For example, they think that prayer in school might improve the deportment of children. At best, that is conjecture, and I question whether it is true. I doubt that high school football players who kneel for locker room prayer before a game play any differently than those who do not pray, unless they gain intensity by the belief that God will take sides in the game. For all the effort to keep a granite monument of the Ten Commandments in the lobby of an Alabama courthouse, I doubt that its presence changed the behavior of any litigant or lawyer who walked by it.

If public religion is, in truth, a show of religiosity more than an act of faith, and if its influence on behavior is doubtful, then I wonder why so many people feel so strongly about the importance of religion in the public square. Why would anyone care enough about nonsectarian prayers in schools or granite-inscribed versions of the Ten Commandments in courthouses to hold vigils to promote his cause? Indeed, why is public religion significant enough to amount to a cause?

I think the reason behind this fervor is an understandable concern about the state of values in our society. When the divorce rate is 50 percent and unwed teen pregnancies are 34 percent, when it seems that family entertainment is impossible to find among the obscene, when children have access to drugs, then there is little wonder that many Americans are desperate to restore some measure of decency to our common life, to return to a world which, at least in our memories, was better than what we have today—a world in which religion seemed to have more force in influencing how people live their lives.

So it seems that we live in a godless age, and we feel deeply that we must reverse this; we must restore God, and we seize upon public religion as a way to do this. School prayer, the Ten Commandments, the teaching of creationism or intelligent design and crèches in front of public buildings all become parts of an effort to reverse our moral course and return our country to a time of public decency.

It is a worthy objective. The problem is that public religion is not up to the task. An innocuous prayer has no power to make us more godly. A display of the Ten Commandments will not make us obey the commandments. What public religion can do is create an appearance that faith is a formality contrived to impress people more than God. It can give us something to argue about among ourselves, in political campaigns and in courts. And when it is not merely vacuous, when it slips into the expression of one religious tradition or another, as it did when I read that prayer at Yale, it tells us that even in our common life, we are not one people, but people on one side or another of a sectarian divide.

The practice of religion is an effective antidote to the disease so apparent in our society. People who practice their beliefs will live according to moral and ethical standards their religion teaches them. They will be witnesses against the tawdriness of the culture around them. They will be examples of the people God expects us to be. They will be that because they understand and live by the tenets of their traditions. That is the practice of religion. It is different altogether from the display of public religion.

The Case of Terri Schiavo

The sad case of Terri Schiavo convinced me of the Christian Right's dominance in the Republican Party. In a persistent vegetative state for fifteen years after suffering loss of oxygen to the brain at age twenty-six, Terri had recently become the Christian Right's political cause. Relying on her husband's testimony that she had previously expressed a wish not to receive life support, and finding that her condition was irreversible, a Florida court had ordered removal of her feeding tube, but frantic parents, desperate to keep her hooked up to the equipment, exhausted reviews in the Florida judicial system.

When that failed, her parents, armed with videotape purporting to show Terri smiling as her eyes followed the movement of a balloon, turned to politicians, first in Florida, then in Washington.

In truth, as her autopsy subsequently determined, Terri's brain had shrunk to half its former size and damage had rendered her blind as well as vegetative. But the videotape seemed to show otherwise, causing religious groups to conclude, "They are murdering Terri."

The uproar from Christian conservatives galvanized Republicans into action both in Florida and in Washington. The Florida legislature enacted a law written so that it applied only to Terri, empowering Governor Jeb Bush to "prevent the withholding of nutrition and hydration from the patient." In Washington, the first plan was to issue a subpoena for Terri to appear before a congressional committee. The idea was that any physician who removed the feeding tube would be interfering with the committee's business and subject to punishment for contempt of Congress. Then that plan was abandoned in favor of legislation to confer federal court jurisdiction on the Schiavo case, which had previously been solely a state court matter.

Congress quickly passed the legislation, and on Palm Sunday 2005, President George W. Bush flew from Texas to Washington on Air Force One to sign it into law. However, the federal court foiled the plan when it refused to order reinsertion of the feeding tube.

Well before the Terri Schiavo case, Congress had agreed to the principle that patients can refuse medical treatment at the end of life. In 1990, Senator Daniel Patrick Moynihan of New York and I introduced a bill called the Patient Self-Determination Act. The drafting and effort behind the bill was the work of my legislative assistant, Elizabeth McCloskey, a devout Roman Catholic and a graduate of Yale Divinity School who is now pursuing a Ph.D. at Catholic University. My principal cosponsor, Pat Moynihan, was a close friend in the Senate and a person with a keen sense of values. The legislation, which Congress quickly enacted into law, requires hospitals to provide all patients with information about their right to refuse medical treatment and the availability of living wills and durable powers of attorney. The legislation does not require advance medical directives. It merely tells patients they can make their own decisions about the extent of their medical treatment.

Liz McCloskey arranged for a leading medical ethicist representing each religion's tradition—Protestant, Catholic and Jewish—to speak at the media conference where we announced the legislation. Each made the point that his faith does not require the use of extraordinary means for the purpose of prolonging the act of dying. This principle was not controversial during the legislative process. I understand that, in practice, the Patient Self-Determination Act has worked effectively.

Unfortunately, Terri Schiavo did not have a living will, and she had not executed a durable power of attorney naming someone else to make medical decisions for her in the event of her incapacity. So Florida courts were left with the responsibility of determining her medical condition and what wishes, if any, she had expressed with regard to end-of-life medical treatment. This the courts did in exceptionally lengthy and careful proceedings. The District Court of Appeal of Florida ruled on four separate occasions in favor of allowing the feeding tube to be removed. In one hearing, the probate court heard testimony from five physicians, which prompted the District Court of Appeal to note that it was "likely no guardianship court has ever received as much high quality medical evidence in such a proceeding." The Florida courts did their duty, determining Terri's medical condition and construing her intent. The trial court heard the facts. The appellate court repeatedly reviewed the case. There the matter should have ended. And that's where the extraordinary intervention of the federal government began. Among other politicians, the Senate's majority leader, Bill Frist of Tennessee, entered the controversy. A medical doctor of great renown, and a highly accomplished heart transplant surgeon before entering the Senate, Frist's opinion on medical matters would carry much weight with his colleagues. On the basis of seeing the videotape of Terri and the balloon, Bill Frist challenged the Florida courts' opinion that Terri was, in fact, in a persistent vegetative state. I have a high regard for the ability of Bill Frist, but I cannot imagine a physician making a medical diagnosis without examining the patient unless he had a special need to appeal to the Christian Right.

Shortly after Terri Schiavo's death, public opinion polls showed that a substantial majority of Americans believed that the federal government should not have intervened and that, after her long ordeal, she should have had the blessing of a merciful death. I suspect that countless Americans related the plight of Terri Schiavo to personal experiences of long and agonizing deaths in their own families or to the fear of a terrible end looming in their own lives. Many, if not most, Americans can imagine a fate worse than death, and it is a seemingly interminable process of dying. For them, it is frightening that politicians can find ways to interject themselves into this sad process.

My own life experiences probably don't differ much from those of countless other people who have lost loved ones to the long process of death. As my mother's youngest child, I always thought we had a special love for each other. She was bright and well read, a graduate of Smith College. She often read books aloud to me, and she taught me vocabulary from a word-a-day book. Because she had a good sense of humor and she thought I was funny, we laughed together a lot. Very frequently, she left little notes for me, always signed, "L & K, Mother."

At sixty-six, she broke a hip in an early morning bathroom fall while my dad was on a fishing trip in Canada. My brother Don broke down the bathroom door to get her. That broken hip was the beginning of a long decline that ended with her death twenty-four years later. A series of small strokes together with Alzheimer's left her mind a shadow of what it had been, reducing her days to sitting on a chaise longue watching television, with little or no comprehension of what she saw.

On trips back to St. Louis from Washington, I stayed in the spare bedroom in her apartment and visited with her, sometimes having dinner with her in her bedroom. I am not sure she knew who I was.

It was the end of life that she did not want. In earlier years, she often talked of "growing old gracefully" and "going down with my flags flying." Despite her mental and physical decline, she maintained her dignity, as best she could, throughout her life. She retained an appearance of graciousness, warmly welcoming visitors from her past, even if she did not remember them or comprehend what they were saying.

In the case of my mother, there was no medical crisis that called for a family decision about giving or withholding medical treatment. She simply died. Had there been a crisis and a need for a family decision, I cannot imagine her death being turned into a political football by religious leaders and politicians eager to impose their will on our family.

My father's death was different. He was seventy-four when surgery to remove an intestinal obstruction revealed that his body was riddled with pancreatic cancer. Seven weeks later, he died after several days in a coma. The family had met in my brother Bill's office, and decided that if nothing useful could be done, nothing medically should be done to prolong the act of dying.

I did not handle my dad's death well. In fact, I could not bear it. Instead of being at his bedside, or present in St. Louis to give strength and gain it from my family, I returned to Jefferson City. On the day of Dad's death, I made myself busy renting a truck and driving to Clarence, Missouri, to pick up a surrey for my farm. I loved my dad. He was as warm, encouraging and loving a father as I could imagine. I should have been there at the end. But there are some people I am glad did not muscle their way into my father's final days: Christian activists and their supportive politicians.

I think a lot of us share a fear that we and people we love will lose control of our own destinies at the end of life. A dear woman who worked in my Senate office in Kansas City shared such an experience with me. Her husband of many years was in a hospital, dying of Lou Gehrig's disease, and hospital personnel had been given strict orders that in the event of a medical emergency, he should not receive treatment to extend his life. One morning she arrived at his bedside to find that, in disregard of the instructions, he was being aggressively treated for pneumonia. She phoned me in an agitated state, wondering how she could countermand a treatment the hospital had commenced.

Sally and I have executed living wills and durable powers of attorney making it clear that in the event of terminal illness, we want to be allowed merciful deaths. But we are worried that the same thing that happened to that man in Kansas City could happen to us. We have read articles that report widespread disregard for living wills by hospitals and physicians, or such narrow reading of what those documents say that they are rendered useless. So we fear that our wishes will be ignored and that strangers who do not share our values will end up making the most personal of all decisions for us.

I suspect that my abhorrence of the Terri Schiavo matter was shared by a lot of people, and that their response to the pollsters was much more strongly felt than an expression of casual opinion. I think the Terri Schiavo case triggered widespread fear. Now it was not just physicians trained in aggressive treatment who were imposing their wills on end-of-life decisions; it was religious crusaders backed by the power of the federal government. That the federal government could intervene in the Schiavo case was a threat to all the families who had seen their loved ones suffer through terminal illness. It was a threat to people who were terrified that their own lives might someday be artificially extended in nightmarish circumstances. It was a threat to some of our most heartfelt values. It was Big Brotherism in the extreme, an exercise of the raw and awesome power of the federal government.

Maybe the public's response to the Terri Schiavo case caught politicians by surprise, but I don't think so. Politicians are very astute in gauging what is popular and what is not, and they conduct their own polling to keep in touch with the public mood. With the general public, they shared personal experiences of agonizing final illnesses in their families or among their friends. Surely they were well aware of the acute sensitivity of interjecting themselves into an end-of-life situation. I believe politicians who intervened in the case of Terri Schiavo were not oblivious to the public response, but did so despite the anticipated public response. They intervened to satisfy the demands of their political base: the Christian Right.

They intervened not in the name of principle, but at the expense of principle. They abandoned the principle recognized when Congress passed the Patient Self-Determination Act: that patients at the end of life should not be kept artificially alive against their will. They abandoned the principle that trial courts exist to decide questions of fact, as had the Florida court, and that courts should act without political interference. They abandoned principle by deciding a medical question without any firsthand knowledge of what they were doing. One views with a degree of pathos the role of William Frist, M.D., graduate of Harvard Medical School and potential presidential candidate, who diagnosed a medical condition without examining the patient.

Then there were the breathtaking departures from the principles of the Republican Party. Traditionally, Republicans have been reluctant to involve government in the private lives of the people. But in this instance, Republicans used the power of government in an effort to decide the fate of one individual. Traditionally, where government does act, Republicans have generally deferred to local and state decision making. But in this instance, Republicans determined that wisdom inside Washington's Beltway trumped the considered judgment of the Florida courts. Traditionally, Republicans have favored limiting the power of federal courts. But in this instance, Republicans conferred special jurisdiction on a federal court in the hope of overturning state court decisions.

The enactment of legislation intended to keep Terri Schiavo hooked up to a feeding tube was a stunning victory for the Christian Right in winning control of the Republican Party. Day after day, for weeks, twenty-four-hour news channels carried accounts of prayer vigils in Florida and rallies outside courthouses. Conservative clergy and their allied politicians were guests on numerous talk shows. Claiming that Florida courts were murdering Terri

The Case of Terri Schiavo

Schiavo, conservative religious groups conducted a massive campaign to influence members of Congress. In sum, the effort to keep Terri Schiavo alive artificially became a religious crusade, and Republicans in Washington responded to a core constituency, even though it meant abandoning traditional Republican philosophy. It was a clear case of appealing to the political base at all costs. Public opinion was discarded, as were fundamental principles. For Republicans, no true believers are of greater value than Christian conservatives. In the case of Terri Schiavo, they proved their power.

ABORTION AND JUDICIAL RESTRAINT

I ask myself why it took the plight of Terri Schiavo to recognize the dominance of the Christian Right in the Republican Party. Active participation by Christian conservatives in my party was nothing new. Pat Robertson, Jerry Falwell and Ralph Reed were well known for their outspoken political activism, and churches, both Roman Catholic and evangelical Protestant, had long been the driving forces in the pro-life movement and key supporters of my political campaigns. Why didn't the abortion issue, so central during my entire political career, raise precisely the same concerns in my mind about the place of religion in government as the isolated case of Terri Schiavo?

Maybe the answer is as simple as my own personal interest. Like people in every other walk of life, politicians want to succeed, and for them, success is measured by winning elections. I wanted to win elections, and Missouri's pro-life movement helped me win. In my closest campaign, the 1982 race for reelection to the Senate, support of pro-life people who voted for me mainly because of my opposition to abortion was the difference between winning and losing.

A favorite tactic of my campaigns, one that I knew about and approved, was to paper the parking lots of pro-life churches on Sundays before elections. Volunteers would place fliers stressing my stand against abortion under the windshield wipers of parishioners' cars. Especially in campaign years, I spoke in churches about my pro-life position. Each January, as pro-life groups rallied in Washington to mark the anniversary of *Roe v. Wade*, I spoke to hundreds of enthusiastic Missourians who had made the long bus trip to Washington. I considered them my political base, and like any politician addressing his base, I did not make dry speeches on public policy. I "let 'er rip," pulling out all the stops to fire up the troops. Having taken advantage of the abortion issue for my own political gain for two decades, it certainly deserves comment that I first complained about the rise of the Christian Right when the case of Terri Schiavo came along.

I may be flattering myself by saying that the difference in principle between the Schiavo case and *Roe v. Wade* is not that I had a political stake only in the latter. Both issues were championed by conservative Christians, but while religion was the sole mover behind the political response to Schiavo, religion was not the sole mover in the opposition to *Roe v. Wade*, at least not in the years immediately following that decision. Even legal scholars who favored the outcome of the case thought that *Roe v. Wade* was not well grounded in the Constitution. In their drive to save Terri

Schiavo, the Christian Right was so dominant that it forced Republicans to abandon their basic principles, especially their long insistence on the limited role of federal courts. Ironically, the activist role for the federal court advanced by Christian conservatives in their rush to save Terri Schiavo cut the ground out from under what had been the leading argument against *Roe v. Wade:* that in *Roe* an expansive Supreme Court had exceeded the bounds of judicial restraint.

Many religious people oppose *Roe v. Wade* because they think abortion is tantamount to murder. They reason that life begins at conception, so abortion is the same as killing innocent babies. Since the U.S. Supreme Court has read the Constitution as allowing what Christian conservatives define as murder, the Constitution has to be amended or the Supreme Court has to be changed. It is the end that counts, and for Christian conservatives, the end is stopping abortion.

That is a religious argument based on the belief of some Christians that life begins at conception. That religious belief has provided all the energy of the pro-life movement, which will not let the abortion issue rest as long as they believe that innocent babies are being murdered. But this religious conviction that has fueled the opposition to legalized abortion has no relation to the constitutional arguments against *Roe v. Wade.* The constitutional arguments pertain not to when life begins, but to the relative powers of state legislatures and the Supreme Court.

State legislatures have broad powers to establish public policy and define public values, as long as they do not violate their own state constitutions or federal law. For example, a legislature can pass laws prohibiting pornography, but those laws cannot be enforced if they violate the constitutionally protected right of free speech. The scope in which a legislature can exercise its powers depends on the limitations placed on it by the Constitution. The more expansive the reading of the Constitution, the more limited the powers of the legislature. Conversely, the tighter the construction of the Constitution, the greater the power of the legislature to define public values. Social conservatives who want to restrict abortion or pornography or protect the family want a legislature strong enough to put their values in legislative form. They do not want a Constitution so broadly interpreted as to prohibit the legislature from protecting the values of the majority as expressed by their elected representatives. Because they want legislatures with the power to implement the values of the majority, they want a narrow and literal construction of the Constitution. Conservatives argue that legislatures are elected by the people and are best able to reflect societal standards. Supreme Court justices are elected by no one, serve for life, and are insulated from the influence of public opinion. Therefore, the values of society are best expressed by the legislative branch of government, not the judicial branch.

I was attorney general of Missouri when the Supreme Court decided *Roe v. Wade*. The job of the attorney general is to defend the laws of the state when they are challenged in court, not to substitute his own opinions on public policy for those of the legislature when it enacted the laws. Missouri has a long, bipartisan history of restrictive statutes on abortion, and a long history of politicians in both parties who opposed abortion. I have no doubt that our politicians accurately expressed the prevailing public sentiment on the issue.

After the Supreme Court decided *Roe v. Wade*, the Missouri General Assembly enacted a new statute, attempting to be as restrictive as possible with respect to abortion without being so restrictive as to run afoul of *Roe v. Wade*. Among other things, the new statute prohibited a particular form of late-term abortion and provided for consent to the procedure by husbands and, in the case of minor children, by parents. As attorney general, I defended the new statute in a case named *Planned Parenthood of Central Missouri v. Danforth*, brought in federal district court to declare the new Missouri statute unconstitutional. As is the practice in declaratory judgment suits, the named defendant was the attorney general. What was unusual was that I personally tried the case before the three-judge district court (presenting, to the consternation of the judges who wanted to hear only the legal arguments, two days of witnesses), and I personally (and unsuccessfully) argued the case when it reached the Supreme Court.

Most of the work of state attorneys general consists of hiring lawyers, making broad decisions and leaving the real legal work to the staff. As attorney general of Missouri, I prided myself on hiring very able, primarily younger lawyers, and giving them responsibility for handling their cases. In the office of another senator, I once saw a framed collection of souvenir quill pens from arguments he had made before the Supreme Court while attorney general of his state. I had made but one such argument, *Planned Parenthood v. Danforth*, preferring to let my assistants have the thrill of arguing before the Supreme Court cases they had handled in lower courts. But *Planned Parenthood* had been mine from the beginning, one of the rare times during my eight years as attorney general that I functioned more as a lawyer than as an administrator.

Why my hands-on approach to this case? Certainly, it was a subject of high visibility, which made it attractive to an elected politician. But beyond that, the case involved what was and remains the most fascinating of all issues of constitutional law: the appropriate limits of the use of judicial power.

At Yale Law School, I had taken a course under one of the great constitutional scholars of the time, and an extraordinarily exciting classroom teacher, Alexander Bickel. The course focused on the extent and limitations of federal court jurisdiction and on legal doctrines courts used to avoid enmeshing themselves in political questions. Because courts exist to decide judicial cases and controversies, and not to appropriate legislatures' prerogatives of creating public policy, the Supreme Court has developed a number of ways to avoid deciding policy disputes. Courts can decline cases if the question is political, if the parties are seeking an advisory opinion, if a party lacks sufficient interest in the outcome to have standing to sue, if the issue is not yet ripe for judicial determination or if the issue is moot. Above all, the role of the court is to interpret the Constitution. It is not to stretch its jurisdiction or to create public policy in the guise of constitutional interpretation.

The Supreme Court decided *Griswold v. Connecticut*, a forerunner to *Roe v. Wade*, while I was in law school. As I recall, we read it as part of Bickel's course. *Griswold* held unconstitutional a Connecticut statute that outlawed the sale of contraceptives, finding in the Constitution a right to privacy that protects from governmental intervention what goes on in the bedroom. I do not recall what Bickel said about *Griswold*. I do remember that I shared the prevailing view at Yale Law School that *Griswold* was an astounding expansion of what the Constitution actually says.

My thought at the time was that in deciding *Griswold*, the Supreme Court was plainly wrong. This had nothing to do with the policy created by the Court. I had nothing against contraceptives; in fact, I approved of them. I liked the idea of a right to privacy, certainly as it applied to the decision of couples to avoid having children. But however laudable these ideas, however desirable it would be to have a right to privacy in the Constitution, I thought that such a right just did not exist. At least I couldn't find it. In my opinion, the Supreme Court had invented a right to privacy, created it out of thin air, and that was a violation of judicial restraint and encroachment into the province of the legislature.

Then came *Roe v. Wade*, building on the new right to privacy and creating the constitutional right to have an abortion, defining to the trimester of pregnancy the limits of state regulation, sweeping aside the considered opinions of state legislatures.

People who oppose abortion on religious grounds believe that a fetus is a human being to be protected from murder. I have not been so certain that a fetus is a person, but I do think that, at some level, it is human life. And if legislatures exist to codify societal values, then it seems to me that legislatures should be able to attribute value to the fetus and enact laws to protect it. Legislatures can protect property from theft and damage by passing criminal laws. In the days of the military draft, Congress prohibited the destruction of a piece of paper: the draft card. I thought that it was within the scope of legislative power to pass such legislation, and I found nothing in the Constitution that said otherwise.

When I argued *Planned Parenthood v. Danforth* in the Supreme Court, just nine days before announcing my candidacy for the Senate, I told the Court that my purpose was not to reopen the case of *Roe v. Wade*. That argument would have had no chance of success. Instead, the issue I presented was whether, after *Roe*, anything remained of traditional areas of state legislative power such as regulating the conditions of marriage and the rights of minor children (spousal consent and parental consent, respectively). The Court held against me, deciding that such traditional legislative powers fell before the new right to have an abortion.

As I saw *Planned Parenthood v. Danforth* and *Roe v. Wade*, the issue before the Court was not religious. It was not the question of when life began. The issue was how broadly the Supreme Court should expand the plain meaning of the Constitution, and thereby contract the power of the legislative branch to embody the will of the people.

Until very recently, the interests of the pro-life movement were congruent with the views of those who believe that courts should construe the Constitution as it is written and as the framers had intended. Pro-life people believed, correctly, that the new right to an abortion was the result of a Court that read its own views of public policy into the Constitution. In their minds, the solution to the problem was the appointment of judicial conservatives to the court. The term "judicial conservative" does not refer to the political views of the potential justice. It has nothing to do with whether the justice is a political conservative, a Republican or even a person who opposes abortion on religious grounds. A judicial conservative is a person who would not embellish the Constitution with his or her personal opinions, whatever those opinions might be.

So when George W. Bush was asked in his campaigns what sort of person he would nominate to fill a vacancy on the Supreme Court, he did not respond that he would nominate someone who would rule against abortion. Instead, he said that there would be no "litmus test" for serving on the Court, and that he would nominate a strict constructionist—someone who would interpret the law, not make it. This answer was all Bush's pro-life supporters needed to hear.

But the real interest of activists, both pro-life and pro-choice, increasingly has been not whether the nominee to the Court was a judicial conservative or a judicial activist, but whether the nominee would vote to overrule *Roe v. Wade*. That has been the trend since the ill-fated nomination of Robert Bork in 1987, when on the day of President Reagan's announcement, Senator Edward Kennedy warned on the Senate floor that Robert Bork's America would mean back-alley abortions. The opposition to the nomination of Clarence Thomas was largely from abortion rights groups that supposed he would be a vote to overrule *Roe v. Wade*.

The unfortunate result of this single-minded focus on the future of abortion rights is that in the public mind, and certainly in the media, the judiciary has joined Congress and the executive as a third political branch of government, existing less to decide questions of law than issues of public policy. Senators subject nominees to extraordinarily repetitious questioning trying to discern how, as individuals, they "feel" about abortion and whether they are "sensitive" to a woman's right to choose. The focus is on a nominee's personal opinions, as though personal opinions do, and should, determine how a justice would decide a matter of law. It is the opposite of what the framers of the Constitution intended when they limited the role of the courts to deciding judicial cases and controversies.

As the decades have passed since *Griswold v. Connecticut* and *Roe v. Wade*, it is increasingly likely that the interests of the pro-life movement are no longer congruent with the views of judicial conservatives. This was clear in the weeks before the Senate confirmed the nomination of Chief Justice John Roberts, a man who is, without a doubt, a judicial conservative. During Senate Judiciary Committee hearings, Roberts stated that he did find a right to privacy in the Constitution, and that he thought that *Roe v. Wade* was "settled law." We cannot be certain how Chief Justice Roberts would decide an abortion case, should one reach the Supreme

Court, but his remarks during the confirmation process seemed to say that his judicial conservatism would point him away from overturning decades of Supreme Court precedent.

The staunch opposition of many on the political and religious Right to the Supreme Court nomination of Harriet Miers showed that judicial conservatism was no longer sufficient to meet their needs. The resignation of Justice Sandra Day O'Connor meant that a swing seat on the Court would be vacant, and they wanted that seat filled by a person who, they thought, would be a committed vote in an abortion case. President Bush tried to assure them that Ms. Miers shared his views on judicial restraint, but that assurance was not enough. So the president took the extraordinary step of saying that Ms. Miers was an evangelical Christian, presumably a comment meant to suggest that she had religious views against abortion that would influence her vote on the Court. That, too, was not enough. Ms. Miers's opponents wanted a known quantity on the Court, someone they could count on to reach the correct results, and Harriet Miers was not a known quantity.

Of course, insistence on a justice who can be counted on to reach the desired result in a case is the opposite of belief in judicial restraint. A determination to impose one's own religious or political views on the law is judicial activism, the very thing pro-lifers said they were against and the very thing I argued against in *Planned Parenthood v. Danforth.*

The heart of the pro-life movement is religiously motivated people determined to end what they see as the morally abhorrent practice of abortion. Their interest is only secondarily in theories of jurisprudence or whether the Supreme Court is activist or restrained. Their interest is in saving the life of the fetus. When judicial activism produced the right to an abortion, pro-lifers were judicial conservatives. As judicial conservatism appears increasingly unlikely to overturn *Roe v. Wade*, they are becoming increasingly activist.

More than thirty years after that decision, I think that it is doubtful that the Supreme Court will overrule itself. And if it did, I doubt that many state legislatures would adopt or continue restrictive abortion laws. But believing they are doing God's work in saving innocent lives, pro-life forces will not soon abandon their cause. Whether judicial conservatism or judicial activism serves their objective, that is the course they will pursue.

STEM CELL RESEARCH

My brother Don teared up when, in the spring of 1999, he told me he had ALS, commonly known as Lou Gehrig's disease. He downplayed the announcement. This was not a sit-down meeting he had prearranged to break the news to me. It was almost as though he said it in passing, after a meeting we had attended in a St. Louis office building, in the garage as we were heading to our cars.

I say he teared up because, although he was emotional when he broke the news to me, he didn't cry. Such tears as were in his eyes were the last I saw in the remaining two years of his life. I cried a lot during those years, often at the worst possible times: when we were talking during a private evening together, when I was standing by his bedside, when I was reading a psalm to him or saying a prayer. I was the well one, supposedly the strong one; but instead of my giving strength to him, he was the one who gave strength to me and to his family and the many people who loved him.

ALS is a disease of the nervous system. It progresses in various ways, starting in Don's case with a slurring of his speech, then a loss of small motor skills, then dramatic weight loss, atrophy of his muscles and loss of the ability to speak and swallow. Throughout his ordeal his mind was sharp, and his personality and wonderful sense of humor were unchanged. People say that the minds of ALS patients are imprisoned in their weakened bodies. That's the way it was with Don.

As his ability to speak declined, he tried to communicate by touching the keyboard of a machine programmed to utter phrases he had picked out. Since our voices were somewhat similar, he asked me to come to his home and say the chosen phrases into the machine, being sure to correct me so that my voice had just the desired inflections. Characteristically, none of the phrases he chose for the machine were about himself; none expressed any self-interest or the slightest self-pity. Every phrase was on the order of "Tell me about yourself."

When the voice machine did not work out to his satisfaction, he began spelling out words by pointing to letters on a board. He did this even on the night of his death, cheering me up by recalling funny things about our childhood.

Don was president of his senior class in high school and captain of the football team. Until his sickness, he was physically strong, and he played tennis and golf, which made his physical decline all the more heart wrenching for those who loved him. He was, as we used to say, a "big deal" as a boy and widely admired as an adult, but his most endearing quality was that he was warm and generous to people who were not big deals at all. He loved little people, and one of the people he loved dearly was his little brother.

He was four years older than I, old enough to treat me with the disdain due a kid brother. Where he was a star high school athlete, I was a gangling klutz. But he stood up for me when big kids teased me, and he let me be his playmate, throwing the baseball around in the backyard or fighting make-believe battles with invisible armies he called specks. We were always playmates, even on the night of his death.

I think of Don every day. I would give anything to have him back.

Numerous scientists at leading research institutions have expressed hope that stem cell research may be the key to discovering cures to ALS and other terrible diseases, including Parkinson's disease and juvenile diabetes. Stem cells are formed at the earliest stages of life, before they begin differentiating into identifiable body parts such as arms and legs. Because they are capable of becoming any part of the body, scientists think that the study of them may provide the answers to diseases that have largely eluded searches for cures, especially diseases of the nervous system.

While stem cells can be harvested from umbilical cords and bone marrow, many scientists insist that it is important to derive them from two other sources that are controversial. One source is frozen embryos in the earliest days of existence, which, if not used, would otherwise be destroyed or eventually deteriorate. These embryos are created in the course of fertility treatments when a physician harvests eggs from a would-be mother, fertilizes the eggs in the laboratory with the father's sperm, and implants some of the eggs in the mother's uterus, freezing the unused embryos in containers of liquid nitrogen.

The second source of stem cells scientists want to pursue is known as somatic cell nuclear transfer technology, or SCNT. This is a process in which a donor's egg is harvested, and its nucleus is removed and replaced by the nucleus from, for example, a skin cell from a potential transplant recipient. This process is believed to be especially promising because the stem cells to be transplanted are less likely than otherwise to be rejected, since they contain the recipient's own genetic material.

One line of attack against SCNT is that this procedure has been used for the reproductive cloning of sheep and other animals, and that it could be used to clone humans. On that point, every reputable scientist I know agrees that the reproductive cloning of humans would be morally reprehensible, and they believe that cloning human beings should result in stiff criminal penalties. But if the goal is to outlaw reproductive cloning, then legislatures should enact statutes that do just that, and they should not take the additional step of outlawing research that can cure disease. To criminalize bank robbery, legislatures outlaw bank robbery. They do not outlaw banks.

While there is nearly universal consensus on criminalizing reproductive human cloning, there is strong disagreement on whether to permit embryonic and SCNT research. Opponents say that embryos, even those that exist outside the womb, and clusters of cells resulting from SCNT procedures are human life. The opponents argue that even if the science is promising, it is wrong to destroy a life to save a life. Clearly, it was morally reprehensible for Nazi doctors to murder Jews for the purpose of medical experimentation. But the assertion that a frozen embryo, discarded during fertility treatment and destined for destruction, is morally indistinguishable from the child next door with juvenile diabetes would not be accepted by many of us and can be explained only on the basis of religious belief.

Attempts to prohibit SCNT are even more clearly religious. Legislation has been introduced at both the federal and state levels to criminalize this type of research—to treat scientists who do it in the same manner as bank robbers—reasoning that the criminal law should be applied to protect human life.

The life in question in SCNT is what is known as a blastocyst, a preembryonic cluster of cells smaller than the period at the end of this sentence. Blastocysts have not been fertilized by sperm, and they will not be implanted in a uterus. Unlike the issue of abortion, where a fetus in the womb will, with the passage of time, become a breathing human being, these cells in a petri dish have no potential other than what scientists can do with them to find cures for diseases. Calling these blastocysts human life can only be understood as a statement of religious doctrine, and advancing legislation to protect them can only be understood as attempting to enforce religion by resorting to the criminal law.

The effect of criminalizing SCNT research would be for the government to protect the blastocyst from research that offers hope to identifiable people. Even if some believe this result to be compelled by their religious convictions, equally devout people would find it an incomprehensible violation of their own values. I heard one person suggest the following hypothetical situation: Suppose you were faced with the choice of whom to save in a burning building. In one room is a three-year-old child. In another room is a petri dish containing a cluster of cells the size of a dot. Which would you rescue from the building, the child or the petri dish?

Now suppose that in one room is a three-year-old child, and in the other is a rack filled with scores of petri dishes. For most people, a single child is of more value than any number of blastocysts.

It's easy to think of hypotheticals to make the point, but a hypothetical is only that. It is no more than a thought, a game played by the imagination. What are more persuasive than the imagined examples we dream up in our minds are our personal experiences of suffering and death of the people who mean the most to us: our families and our friends.

No theologian, however learned; no church council, however authoritative; no bishop or archbishop, however holy will ever persuade me that protecting a frozen embryo that will never see the light of day should take precedence over my brother Don. No religious doctrine, however earnestly formulated, will ever convince me that cells in a laboratory are so significant that my brother should be denied the benefits of medical research. The very notion goes against both my reason and my deepest feelings. The notion that people with different religious views could co-opt politicians to the point of enacting their beliefs into law is more than offensive. It is a misuse of government to advance religion. It is a clear breach in the separation of church and state.

Admittedly, my experience of watching the steady progression of ALS as it destroyed my brother's body and took his life affects my opinion of stem cell research, so what I say could be discounted as merely personal. Yes, it is personal, but that's just the point. On one hand, we have the religious theory that life exists even before it is implanted in the uterus, that life in the laboratory is of such value that it demands the protection of the state. On the other, we have the personal experiences of all sorts of people who have watched their loved ones suffer and die.

Compare the blastocyst to the Alzheimer's patient. For those of us who are middle aged or older, who among us has not known once proud and happy people stricken with this disease—people who after many years of decline can only stare vacantly into space? We have known them in their better days, lived with them, laughed with them, worked with them. Now we see them, and there is nothing there, no glimmer of recognition or understanding. And we live in terror that the same end will come to us.

At least Alzheimer's patients do not know what is happening to their brains and bodies. Some say this makes Alzheimer's less terrible than ALS, where the patient understands everything. But if lack of comprehension is of some small blessing to the Alzheimer's victim, it does nothing to help the family. Care of the stricken spouse or parent can consume a family's time, energy and resources. Instead of enjoying retirement years, a husband or wife, whose own strength may be declining with age, can find every day consumed by care giving. Then there is the wrenching decision of whether to place the loved one in a nursing home, a decision that can result in enormous cost, not to mention guilt.

While spouses of Alzheimer's victims hope for medical breakthroughs, scientists tell me that because of the complexity of the disease, finding its cure is much less promising and more remote in time than treatment of other diseases. Stem cells have been used successfully to cure Parkinson's in monkeys, and one scientist told me that the treatment of humans could be just a few years away.

So many people have suffered from ALS, Parkinson's, juvenile diabetes and other diseases, or have witnessed it in their families, that the demand for cures will overcome the resistance of those who would ban stem cell research. When I was in the Senate, legions of blind people once arrived at the U.S. Capitol to demand the end to a federal regulation denying them seating in exit rows in airplanes. Congress responded with urgency. In the same way, associations representing various disease groups will mobilize their members to oppose restrictions on stem cell research. What is surprising is not that the supporters of research will eventually prevail, but that the opponents of embryonic and SCNT research were able to persuade President Bush and a number of members of Congress and state legislatures to support their point of view.

The explanation is that pro-life churches have been more effective than, for example, the Juvenile Diabetes Association in communicating with politicians. In April 2005, a postcard-sized form was distributed at Catholic churches throughout the state of Missouri:

> I urge you as my elected state legislator, to protect the sanctity of life for all human beings. As a pro-life constituent, I support research using stem cells from nonembryonic sources. PLEASE SUPPORT A BAN ON ALL HUMAN CLONING. SUPPORT SB 160. SUPPORT HB 457. I urge you to take up for debate and pass SB 160 and HB 457.

In using the highly charged words "human cloning," the postcard is misleading, confusing the universally condemned notion of reproducing cloned human beings with research related to finding cures for diseases. But more telling than the misleading words of the postcard is the point of distribution: churches. Opposition to SCNT and early stage embryonic stem cell research is the official position of the Catholic church in Missouri. By order of the bishops, a ballot initiative permitting such research has been opposed in homilies delivered in every Catholic church in the state.

It is a basic right of Americans to communicate with politicians in whatever manner they choose, and to express any idea they wish. If our opinion is based on religious convictions, it is as welcome in our political life as any other opinion. Stem cell research is one issue among many where religious people have felt called to express their beliefs to those who represent them in government. In that sense, it is no different from abortion, civil rights, the death penalty and other issues where religious people have attempted to influence public policy.

What distinguishes the opposition to embryonic stem cell research and SCNT is that it is based solely on a religious belief that life begins before implantation in the uterus. This religious concept is in opposition to the convictions of other people of faith who do not share this definition of the beginning of life, and who believe that it is their own religious obligation to discover the cures for disease, to heal the sick, to relieve suffering and to save lives.

Legislators considering banning such research should realize that they are being asked to establish one religious point of view and to oppose another.

GAY MARRIAGE

A few years ago, a woman who had moved back to Missouri after working in my Senate office arranged to meet my plane when I flew into her hometown. Bright, personable and attractive, with a wonderful sense of humor, she added joy to our office, and I looked forward to seeing her again and catching up with what was going on in her life. With her sunny disposition and keen appreciation for the ridiculous, I was certain I was in for an enjoyable half hour or so as she drove me to my destination. Instead, just as we were leaving the airport, she said that she had something to tell me, and that she hoped I would not be disappointed in her. Then she told me she is gay. How ironic the word sounded. She was gay, and she was in tears. She said that she was in love with another woman. I asked her to tell me about the other woman, to tell me if she was a good person. I asked her if she was happy. Yes, she answered, the other woman was very good, and she was very happy.

I did not have to ask her why she was crying if she was happy. She had already told me the reason. She thought of me as a father figure, and she was anxious about how I would react. I assured her that if she was happy, I was happy for her. For me, it was a window into understanding how a lot of gay people think. Even when they are at home with their own sexuality, by not accepting them, the world around them has the capacity to make them miserable.

A few years after graduation, a high school classmate of mine committed suicide. I do not know why, and I do not know if he was gay, but I have wondered since if he felt that the society around him would never accept him. In those days, now fifty years ago, homosexuality was an object of contempt and derision. Hate crimes against gays continue to occur, and gay people continue to face hatefulness in our society. I know my friend who picked me up at the airport that day had sufficient concern about being rejected that she burst into tears. I know that I want no part in the meanness that causes this kind of misery.

Until the last year or so of my time in the Senate, I was unaware that the lives of gay citizens were a political issue. If gay civil rights groups existed, they were not visible to me, nor were any efforts by the Christian Right to politicize sexual orientation. It was a nonissue and had I thought about it, its remaining a nonissue would have been fine with me. I have never wanted to offend gays, or say or do anything to hurt them. Still, they were objects of public contempt, so as a politician concerned about his own popularity, I did not want to be seen as their friend. This was so even at the end of my political career after I had announced that I would not run for reelection. I had nothing to lose as far as political support was concerned, but I never lost my craving for popularity. With only a little more than a year to go before retirement from the Senate, the issue of gay civil rights burst into my political life.

The occasion was a 1993 trip to Washington in which gays from across the country traveled to the Capitol to meet members of Congress. I had learned in advance that several hundred people were coming from Missouri and that they wanted a meeting with me, where they would be accompanied by media from the state. A lot of groups come to Washington every year to press their agendas on Congress, so the idea of a large contingent arriving from Missouri was nothing new. What was new was that this was a group of gay constituents, and the meeting would be reported in my home state's media. It was not the sort of coverage I wanted.

I had an out—a perfectly understandable excuse for avoiding the meeting. Because this was the first large-scale gay trip to Washington, it had not been very well planned. The group arrived not on a day when the Senate was in session, and senators could be expected to be in their offices, but on a federal holiday—I think it was Columbus Day—when the Senate was not meeting and when very few senators were around the Capitol. In fact, I had not planned to be in that day; and when we realized that the Senate was not in business, politically minded members of my staff and I breathed sighs of relief that I would be spared this unwelcome media event.

Except, convenient as the excuse seemed, availing myself of it just did not seem right. Hundreds of constituents had made the effort to come to Washington, and they came there, in part, to see their senators. So I went to the Capitol and met with the group from Missouri in one of the Senate committee rooms.

The setting of the meeting emphasized the serious nature of my constituents' purpose. Committee rooms in the Dirksen Senate Office Building are dark, cavernous halls where wood paneling absorbs much of the light that comes through their windows. They are gloomy places where no one would want to be on the morning of a holiday weekend, especially after having flown half way across the country to spend less than an hour with a senator. Yet a large number of Missourians had sufficient commitment to their beliefs to spend their Columbus Day in just such a room.

I stood in front of the horseshoe-shaped rostrum where senators normally sit, and invited the thoughts of the large group seated before me.

In my memory, it was a cordial meeting, with only one point of difference between my visitors and me. Someone asked if I favored amending the federal law that forbids employment discrimination on the basis of race, religion and gender to include sexual orientation as well. I answered that I opposed such legislation, which was not the answer they wanted to hear. At the time, I did not think that discrimination on the basis of sexual orientation was comparable to other kinds of discrimination. I thought then that homosexuality, as contrasted to race, gender and religion, was merely a matter of personal preference that an individual could change at will. I reasoned that while the power of government should be used to protect what I considered basic civil rights, employers should be able to accept or reject matters of lifestyle without government coercion.

Moreover, although I was near retirement from the Senate,

I remained a politician who realized that support for the legislation would have caused a clamor in Missouri, not only from people who were contemptuous of gays, but also from businesspeople who did not want any more government regulations about whom they could hire. In the eyes of businesspeople, many of whom had been my supporters, I had done quite enough by sponsoring major legislation governing employment discrimination two years earlier.

With an eye toward the attending media and the uproar I imagined I might cause back home by answering otherwise, I told the questioner that I did not favor expanding the statute, and that employers should be able to make up their own minds on sexual orientation as a criterion of employment. Today, I would give a different answer. Today, I believe that homosexuality is a matter of sexual orientation rather than preference. It is not merely a choice of lifestyle. Discrimination on the basis of sexual orientation is, in my view, comparable to discrimination on other civil rights grounds. It is wrong, and it should be prohibited by law.

The *St. Louis Post-Dispatch* was among the local media represented in that committee room, and it soon ran a long story about the group of gay constituents coming to Washington. Buried in that story was a brief account of my position at that time on employment discrimination based on sexual orientation. Sometime after the article appeared, I received a long letter from a lay leader of Christ Church Cathedral in St. Louis, the cathedral of my home diocese. The letter stated that, as reported in the *Post-Dispatch*, my remarks in Washington had been insensitive to gays and "hurtful," and that members of the cathedral had been meeting to consider ousting me as a canon, an honorary cathedral position I had been given a number of years earlier. I responded with a long letter of explanation that seemed to satisfy the people I had offended, and I heard nothing more about the idea of removing me as a canon.

To me, the message from Christ Church Cathedral was astonishing, even maddening. I could not imagine anyone thinking anything I said was insensitive or hurtful. I do not intentionally go around hurting people, making them feel bad about themselves, and that was certainly not my purpose when I met with my constituents in Washington. My answer to the question about employment discrimination was undoubtedly politically calculated, but it was not calculated to hurt. That people took it that way was a learning experience for me. Political issues are not abstractions. The ways in which they are presented affect the ways human beings think about themselves. What might seem a benign comment by the speaker might be very harmful to the listener. When I met with them in Washington, people who had been insulted and sometimes brutalized by the straight world for most of their lives were understandably attuned to hearing hurtful words, even when no hurt was intended.

The capacity to be offended at the words and actions of others is not the monopoly of gays. Many straight people thought that the recent spate of same-sex weddings on city hall steps in San Francisco and New Paltz, New York, was a media circus and a parody of the institution of marriage.

After I raised the issue of the straight perception of these city hall weddings at a St. Louis meeting of the Log Cabin Republicans, an organization that works to create better understanding between gays and the Republican Party, I received a very thoughtful letter from a friend who had attended the meeting. He said he did not think gays intended to give offense by these ceremonies. He wrote, "I think what we saw was an incredible out-pouring of jubilation from people who were finally being allowed to do what they had wanted to do for years." My friend's letter reminded me of my own reaction when told that my remarks had hurt the group of gay constituents who had visited me in Washington. On emotionally charged issues, it is natural that we are quick to take offense at what other people say or do. That is why it is important to try to understand what we are seeing and hearing, and not to take offense where no offense is intended.

There is no doubt in my mind that the vast majority of Americans, gay and straight, have no intention of hurting one another, and that if allowed to do so, without the premature intervention of courts, the opportunistic interference of politicians and the divisive interference of religious leaders, the vast majority of Americans would work out, in a mutually respectful way, how they deal with issues of sexual orientation. I believe the broad outlines of such an agreement would include the following:

- Establishment of the principle that discrimination in all forms, including sexual orientation, is wrong and should be unlawful;
- Governmental recognition of committed same-sex relationships, including the creation of legal status with regard to property rights, pension benefits, insurance and inheritance;
- Development by religious groups of ways to bless committed same-sex relationships;
- A strong emphasis on the importance of committed, long-term relationships and the disavowal of sexual permissiveness, whether straight or gay;

- The honoring of traditional marriage between a man and a woman.

It would require a conscientious effort by both sides to create a common approach to gay issues, and even the approach I have outlined has omitted at least one hot-button issue: the adoption and custody of children. What I do believe is that most Americans could work out an accommodation on these matters if they had the opportunity to do so. But nothing has matched gay marriage as an example of the emotional heat created by the mixture of religion and politics.

Gay marriage burst into national prominence on November 18, 2003, when the Supreme Judicial Court of Massachusetts ruled that under the state's constitution, same-sex couples have the same right to marry as straight couples. It was a remarkable example of judicial activism in the extreme. A court prematurely interjected itself into a question of societal values, and transformed an issue which might well have been resolved through evolving social standards into a fight over fixed constitutional principles.

But if the action of the Massachusetts court was bad, the political response to it was worse. While the case was pending, Congresswoman Marilyn Musgrave of Colorado introduced a resolution in the United States House of Representatives that would have amended the U.S. Constitution to state that "marriage in the United States shall consist only of the union of a man and a woman." One week after the Massachusetts court decision, Senator Wayne Allard, also of Colorado, introduced an identical resolution in the Senate. In both the House and the Senate, more than 90 percent of the members cosponsoring the proposed constitutional amendment were Republicans.

Meanwhile, at the state level, opponents of same-sex marriage have been at least as active as members of Congress. In 2004, eleven states amended their own constitutions to ban same-sex marriage. Thirty-seven state legislatures have passed statutes to the same effect.

The rapid response of Republican politicians was urged by the outcry of conservative Christian leaders against same-sex marriages. Dr. James Dobson, founder and chairman of the conservative organization Focus on the Family, was especially colorful in his commentary:

"Saying there's a constitutional guarantee for two homosexuals to marry is just a few steps away from saying there's a constitutional guarantee to marry more than one person, or for relatives to marry, or even for people to marry their pets. What makes this a truly dark day is that gay marriage is only the beginning."

In another statement, Dobson said that after the Massachusetts court decision "the homosexual activist movement . . . is now closer than it has ever been to administering a devastating and potentially fatal blow to the traditional family."

Disagreement with the Massachusetts court is not enough to warrant amending the Constitution of the United States. The Constitution defines the structure of the federal government and its relationship to the people. It does not create social policy. Prohibition, the one exception to writing personal behavior into the Constitution, was such a failure that it was repealed thirteen years after its adoption. Issues of social policy, if handled by government at all, are better left to the more responsive legislative branch, preferably at the state level, than enshrined in the Constitution, where they will be interpreted and applied by the courts. What is more, it seems bizarre that the subject of gay marriage would appear in the Constitution alongside freedom of speech and due process of law.

If we are to consider amending the Constitution, we should have very persuasive reasons for doing so. The arguments for the proposed marriage definition amendment are so far-fetched as to be comical. Let's consider the statements of Dr. James Dobson.

First, he argues that "gay marriage is only the beginning" and that constitutional guarantees for polygamy, incest and bestiality are "just a few steps away." Come on. None of us can reasonably feel threatened that even the most activist court would uphold a right to multiple spouses, or incest or, as Dr. Dobson puts it, the right of people "to marry their pets." Every now and then we read stories about tiny religious sects in remote areas that practice polygamy, but it is unimaginable that these weird little outposts threaten the decency of the nation. Nor can we imagine parades of men pounding on courthouse doors, demanding to marry their sisters. And as much as we Americans love our pets, it is laughable to suggest that the day may come when people will want to marry their dogs, or cats, or canaries. The slippery-slope argument, that same-sex marriage is only the first step toward all sorts of deviancy, is just plain silly.

Second, Dobson fears that same-sex marriage threatens "a devastating and potentially fatal blow to the traditional family." This argument has gained favor with members of Congress who style legislative efforts against same-sex marriage as "defense of marriage" laws.

America's divorce rate is now 50 percent, and marriage is under attack from a number of quarters: finances, promiscuity, alcohol and drugs, the pressures of work, cultural acceptance of divorce, et cetera. But it is incomprehensible that one of these threats is when someone else, whom we have never seen, in a place where we may never have been, has done something we don't like. As a practical matter, by prohibiting a same-sex marriage in Boston, Congress in Washington would do nothing to protect a heterosexual marriage in St. Louis.

In addition to the two arguments Dr. Dobson advances for a constitutional amendment, I have heard one other, which is as follows: A same-sex couple might marry in Massachusetts and move to Missouri. Under the United States Constitution, Missouri would be forced to recognize the marriage and pay the same-sex spouse "taxpayers' money" pursuant to some benefit program. So, it is said, people in states that do not approve of same-sex marriage would be forced, against their will, to support same-sex couples.

At most, this would involve an infinitesimal burden on Missouri taxpayers. Consider the assumptions behind the argument: (1) some significant number of same-sex couples would marry in Massachusetts, or some other place that allows such marriages; (2) a significant percentage of such couples would migrate to Missouri; (3) a significant number of such people would qualify for some unspecified state benefit by reason of spousal status; and (4) the state would not contest making such payments. Whatever few pennies such a chain of events would extract from the pockets of any single taxpayer of Missouri would surely not warrant the drastic step of amending the Constitution.

No doubt the issue of same-sex marriage is of great importance to gay couples living in committed relationships who would like the broader society to validate and honor their relationships. I think society and churches should find ways to do that, whether or not they call it marriage. While I do not agree with the Supreme Judicial Court of Massachusetts, I do not think the proposed constitutional amendment defining marriage could possibly accomplish any of the objectives claimed by its supporters.

For this reason, I think that the only purpose served by the campaign for the amendment is the humiliation of gay Americans, advocated by the Christian Right and eagerly supported by its suitors in the Republican Party. To call it a constitutional amendment designed to defend marriage makes it seem something loftier than gay bashing. But in reality it is gay bashing.

* * *

On the same day I am sending this book to press, a test vote in the U.S. Senate has rejected the proposed Marriage Protection Amendment to the Constitution, which would have defined marriage as the union of a man and a woman. Despite the strong endorsement of President Bush, only forty-nine senators supported the amendment, far short of the sixty-seven required for a constitutional amendment. Forty-seven Republicans supported the amendment and seven opposed it. The failure to win even a simple majority in the Senate has prompted widespread commentary that the real purpose of the proposal was to energize the Republican base before the 2006 midterm election. In an interview the day before the Senate vote, Dr. James Dobson said, "It is true what this vote will do is help voters identify who is and who is not supportive of the family. And I think those that are not are going to have to answer for it."

FAMILY VALUES

S oon after the 2004 election, I wrote President George W. Bush a letter resigning as America's ambassador to the United Nations, wording the letter so that it would remove me from consideration for any full-time position in the administration. In part, the letter said, "After a lot of thought and prayer, Sally and I have decided to return to private life, hopefully beginning January 20, 2005.

"I want you to know how much I appreciate the opportunity to serve the United States at the United Nations. It has been an important time to be in this position, especially as we attempt to enlist greater U.N. participation in the future of Iraq, and as we advance the interest you have personally shown in helping the desperate people of Sudan. I am proud to be part of your administration.

"Forty-seven years ago, I married the girl of my dreams, and at this point in my life, what is most important to me is to spend more time with her. Because you know Sally, you know my reason for going home."

Ever since my resignation became public, many people have approached me, asking me to confide in them the "real" reason I left government. Some have said, with understanding nods, that they know the real reason, even though I had refrained from stating it, the assumption being that I had quit in protest over some disagreement about the course of the administration's foreign policy. In fact, the reason for leaving government was precisely as stated in the letter: After forty-seven years of marriage, it seemed important for me to spend more time at home with Sally.

The term "family values" is generally understood to mean a political agenda, a set of issues championed by the Christian Right on subjects including opposition to abortion and gay marriage, but a more literal meaning might have less to do with positions on the issues than with the degree to which the politician values family. In short, what are his or her priorities? Does the politician think and speak of a life in politics as though politics is the context in which the rest of life is lived, or is her or his politics a part of a larger life that gives it the perspective of other interests?

Practicing religion entails setting priorities. Jesus made it clear that his followers should leave family, even hate family, for the sake of the kingdom of heaven. So if the politician believes that the kingdom of heaven is advanced by a political agenda, that God's truth is known and can be reduced to government policy, then no concern for family should interfere with the politician's pursuit of God's cause. All ambitious people face difficult choices between the competing demands of career and family. For the politician who believes he is on a mission from God, the demands of career are especially preemptive.

But if the work of the politician is more modest, if the politician lacks certainty that he possesses God's truth, if he sees himself as struggling to be faithful but never able to embody God's will in his politics, the claim of family over work is more pressing. In the Bible, the primary claim for family loyalty is by the spouse.

Genesis tells us that a man leaves his father and mother and "cleaves" to his wife. The dictionary definition of cleave is "to adhere to firmly and closely or loyally and unwaveringly." My own mental image of cleaving is the bonding together of two objects, say the gluing of two pieces of wood so that they are as one. All the instructions I have seen on the subject say that it is important to clean the surfaces of the two objects before applying the glue so that external matter does not interfere with the bonding. For me, this is a metaphor for marriage because all sorts of external influences, people as well as interests, interpose themselves between the marital partners. That is the case for every married couple. The external influence may be, as the verse in Genesis suggests, the claims on a husband or wife by demanding parents, or it may be the responsibilities of raising children, or the hours and energy devoted to one's job. The challenge for every married couple is to cleave together and not allow the external influences that insert themselves into the marriage to break the bond between them.

In the marriage of a politician, and most definitely in the marriage of a United States Senator, the job is especially intrusive in the marriage. It is not only that the job requires long work days and a lot of travel, but that it carries with it the powerful message that marriage and family come second. "Will you be home for dinner?" "I don't know; it depends on the Senate's schedule." "Will you attend the school play?" "I don't know; it depends on the Senate's schedule." Wife and children may fit into a senator's life, but only when the Senate's schedule permits them to do so. Then there are the constant assurances a senator receives of the supreme importance of the job, the momentous nature of every legislative effort, the brilliance of every utterance, assurances from obsequious Senate functionaries and lobbyists and from the senator's own self-congratulatory press releases. The implication is that anything that goes on within the home pales in significance compared to what takes place in the Capitol.

How any senator deals with the intrusiveness of the office into family life varies with the individual. In describing my own case, I am aware that what I say will seem self-serving, but I will try to be straightforward, drawing on my own thoughts as well as the memories my wife and five children have shared with me. In my own mind, my priorities were always clear. Sally came first; then the children; then my roots, including family tradition and sense of belonging to a place, Missouri; then my political life.

No one in life has given me more joy, more of a sense of wholeness than Sally. We are two parts of one person. We know each other's thoughts, complete each other's sentences, sense each other's happiness or hurt before a word is said. And we say a lot of words. When we are in a car or at a table, we talk. The subjects may be serious or frivolous. They are often repetitious. And we chatter away like a couple of magpies. We touch each other; we hold hands; we hug; we laugh, a lot, until tears run down our cheeks. We accept each other's weaknesses and admire each other's strengths. We complete each other. When I am away from Sally, I long for her, always counting the days, often the hours until I will see her again. We dread the loss of each other.

Our children all speak with great feeling about the closeness of Sally and me. They say that during my years of public life they never heard her express a word of complaint about the demands of my job. Sally and the children say that despite those demands, they never doubted that in my heart, they came before my career.

Eleanor, our oldest daughter, is now in her mid forties. Her first memory of knowing I was in politics was at a Girl Scout campout after we had moved to Jefferson City, when she was in fourth grade. She describes herself as a new kid in town who was shy and awkward. Another girl approached her and said, "You think you're so great because your dad is attorney general." Eleanor recounts that she was "floored," that she did not know what an attorney general was, and that she thought we had moved to Jefferson City because I had a new job. As she puts it, "You were my dad." Our third daughter, D.D., recalls her first political memory from when she was in first grade, and she was aware that I was running for re-election. She supposes she saw a HELP WANTED sign, which comforted her. She thought that if I lost my job as attorney general, I could get a job in a gas station. All of our children mention the importance of the family dinner table, never a time for television, when I asked each child to tell about the events of the day, and seldom talked about politics or the Senate.

My consistent theme during the Senate years was that Washington was my work station, but it was not our home. As our daughter Mary puts it, it was always clear that we would leave. "When this is over, we're out of here." Our children knew of an idea I had borrowed from my childhood. When I visited Purina feed mills with my father, I saw pictures of typical farmers, and beneath each picture was the legend "The Boss." After I was elected to the Senate, I asked Bob Lindholm, an excellent photographer and an assistant attorney general, to take a photograph of someone he considered a representative Missourian. For the next eighteen years, that photograph hung behind my desk in my Senate office, an elderly man in a seed cap and bib overalls, staring straight at me, and under the picture the words "The Boss."

We were not Washingtonians. I answered to the Boss, the people of Missouri. We were Cardinals fans, both baseball and football. I would not root for the Redskins, and I encouraged my children not to do so either. While this reinforced the belief that wife, children and roots came before the Washington life of a senator, it had the negative effect of detaching the family, especially the children, from the community in which we lived. Mary, who now lives in St. Louis with her family, has commented on the difference between living in St. Louis and the detached way I led our family to consider our presence in Washington. "In St. Louis, when someone is sick, you take them muffins or a chicken. In Washington, there was none of that. It wasn't a good model for adult friendships."

My resolve that the family think of itself as rooted in Missouri, and my insistence that we never become fans of Washington sports teams, cost our son, Tom, the joy of sharing common interests with his schoolmates and with his dad. We seldom went to games together, and if we did, we didn't go as fans for the home team. We did not sit on the family room couch and scream at the television set about sports. Still, Tom felt duty bound to me to remain a Missourian. The then generally hopeless St. Louis football Cardinals seldom won against the dominant Washington Redskins, but one Sunday was a rare exception. The next morning, Tom, in grade school, arrived at the breakfast table done up in Cardinals regalia. I told Tom that it might not be a good idea to show up at school that way, especially since the Redskins would probably win the next time the teams met. Tom said, "I don't care, I'm going to school and I'm going to say, 'Cardinals won, Redskins lost.'" This was followed by a loud raspberry. Rooting for the wrong sports team seems like a small thing, but losing a sense of belonging to a community for the sake of pleasing your father is not a small thing.

It is reasonable to question how a story about my son's experience with his schoolmates, or any other account of my family life, could be relevant to a book about faith and politics. What is deeply personal and important to my wife, our children and me may seem disconnected from anything pertinent to the public interest. This point would be apt were the political implications of faith merely a set of policy positions one could deduce from religious principles. In that event, family matters would be beside the point in a discussion of faith and politics. On the other hand, if my basic premise is correct, how a politician combines family life and political life is very relevant. Unlike the Christian Right's, my premise is that faith does not lead us inexorably to a set of public policies, and that the creation of a political agenda in the name of religion soon becomes divisive and can easily slip into idolatry. That, I believe, is the case with the family values initiative.

While, in my opinion, faith does not provide us with a specific political agenda, it does guide faithful people in their approach to politics and in the values they carry with them into the public square. In that context, I have thought about family values in my own life. To help me in that thinking, I have asked the experts: my family.

Our children are unanimous in saying that despite their sense of not belonging to Washington, they believed that their lives were normal. They were puzzled by questions they sometimes heard: "Do you have a driver?" "Does your dad have a driver?" "Does your dad have a bodyguard?" The answer to each of these was no. The four youngest children, who grew up in Washington, did not feel that they particularly stood out in a city of high-profile people. Sally, who is naturally down to earth and who did not complain to them about my work, helped create the belief that we were a normal family living normal lives.

But while Sally did not complain to the children, it was clear to her and to me that my Senate career did intrude on, preempt and sometimes devalue the person I loved more than any job or any thing.

Every five or six weeks, the Senate recessed for a week, meaning that with the addition of a weekend, attendance in Washington would not be necessary for about ten days. To people outside the Senate, that seems like a very easy schedule—a one-week vacation every month or so. Except that it was not a vacation. It meant returning to the state for much of the time, traveling from town to town, seeing constituents and leaving the family behind. For two or three days before those trips, Sally would become withdrawn from me and sometimes testy, a change in mood often culminating with Sally crying in bed on the night before my departure. As strong believers in the biblical admonition not to let the sun set on our anger, we talked and cried the matter out until Sally was resigned to my going. It was not just that I was leaving, although we have never liked being apart, but that I was leaving her behind. I was going off to the state, while she was staying in Washington with the responsibilities of children and home. I was having the interesting life, and she was coming in second. I would return from trips, or even from a day in the Senate, exhausted, uninterested in anything stimulating to her, and she would be left with, as she put it, "the dregs." It was not what marriage should be.

When in session, I would call her up, say at six o'clock. "The Senate may be out in an hour, maybe later. Who knows? Save dinner for me." But despite the importance we attached to sharing the dinner hour with our children, Sally's efforts to have us eat together often did not work out. So Sally might end up fixing three dinners—one for the younger children, one for the older children, one for me. My job was doing more than keeping her off balance; it was jerking her around. And in Sally's mind, if not in the minds of our children, it was usurping the attention she should be giving to them.

When Eleanor graduated from the University of Virginia, she landed her first job at the Washington headquarters of the Peace Corps. She and Sally had bought new clothes for her work, and the day before her first day, she made a test run on the bus to learn how to get to the office on time. On the afternoon of what was to be Eleanor's first day at her new job, Sally arrived home to find her crying in the backyard of our house. The job had lasted only a matter of hours. Peace Corps director Loret Ruppe had fired Eleanor on learning that she was my daughter. She could not keep her because she had political connections. I came home just after Sally, and told her that we were running late and had to leave for a fundraiser someone was holding for my forthcoming campaign. As Sally sees it, instead of giving comfort and reassurance to our daughter who had been fired, she had to be nice to strangers at a fund-raiser. She has said, "I was doing something really wrong, and I knew it."

Sally and Tom remember election night of 1982. Early in that very tense evening at a dinner with family and close campaign workers, the mood was somber because we thought I had lost my race for reelection to the Senate. When it turned out that I had won, our family left the dinner for the victory celebration in a hotel ballroom. Sally recalls that we were standing on the stage when she noticed Tom, then ten years old, crying. He thought I had lost. As Sally sees it, we were so caught up in the excitement of the election that we neglected our son and failed to tell him I had won.

About once a week, Sally and I went to dinners, often fascinating evenings in homes where the guests were leading figures in politics and the media. Occasionally, they were command performances, black-tie political events that no reasonable person would voluntarily attend. When the Senate was expected to be working late, I would take my tuxedo to the office and change. Sally would put on an evening dress and jewelry at home, and take a taxi to the Capitol to meet me. On one such evening, the taxi carrying Sally stopped on the way to the Capitol to pick up additional passengers. They were two strippers—one woman, one man. They asked Sally her name, and she was too polite not to tell them. They began commenting on her jewelry, on her purse, on her evening dress—all the time calling her by her name. They put their hands on her arms, her legs, her body. She felt powerless to stop them. It was an unpleasant and outrageous experience, but what makes it noteworthy is what happened after the taxi finally delivered Sally to my office. She wanted the comfort of my arms and my words. She began to recount her experience, "You won't believe what happened." But I was not alone. Some of my Senate staff were with me, and they cut her off before she could tell me, briefing me about some Senate issue as I was putting the studs in my tuxedo shirt. Sally recalls that she felt invisible. She asked herself, "What am I doing here?" And followed up to herself, "I want to go home to my mother."

Sometimes the devaluation of Sally was thoughtless, as it was that evening in my Senate office. Once it was physical. As Sally was handing out campaign literature outside a St. Louis supermarket, a woman shopper punched her in the stomach. Once it was crude. At the annual state Republican gathering known as Lincoln Day, officeholders and candidates are expected to have hospitality suites to entertain party activists. One year we made the mistake of having our own hotel bedroom be part of the hospitality suite. When we returned to the bedroom after the last guest had left, we found a cigar butt in Sally's shoe and a four-letter expletive scrawled in Sally's lipstick on the bathroom mirror.

Much more common were ways in which people treated Sally as though she did not exist or did not count. Very often we would be standing together at an event when someone would walk up to me and engage me in conversation, turning his back on Sally.

One of the great people we knew in Washington was Katharine Graham, publisher of the *Washington Post*. She was smart, interesting and kind, and she was our friend. At the reception after her funeral, one of the guests said that Kay Graham had "convening authority" in Washington. That she did. Dinners in her Georgetown home were gatherings of Washington's most powerful people, and opportunities to exchange information and ideas and build bipartisan bridges. At one such evening, a well-known newspaper woman asked Sally, "What do you do?" When Sally replied, "I raise five children," the newspaper woman turned her back and walked away. What made that experience ironic was that minutes later, at dinner, Sally was sitting between a cabinet member and the editor in chief of a national weekly magazine, holding her own on the issues of the day.

I valued Sally, but some of the circumstances of my career did not. Our time in Washington was during the height of the women's movement, and Sally was not happy with the role of, as she called it, "wife of." A popular song of the time was Helen Reddy's "I Am Woman," which Sally played on her car's tape deck as she sang along to the lyrics: "I am woman, hear me roar." But instead of roaring, she felt secondary to me—pleasing me, pleasing our children, pleasing the people of Missouri but not fulfilling herself. In blue periods, she closed herself in a room and wrote poetry, long since destroyed, that was never seen by another soul—poetry about the empty feeling of her life.

I do not mean that Sally was relentlessly depressed, for she was not. She enjoyed the stimulus of Washington, the intellectually exciting dinners in the homes of Katharine Graham, Meg Greenfield, Rollie and Kay Evans, Henry and Jessica Catto and many others. She read the *Washington Post* cover to cover to keep up with current events. She enjoyed state dinners at the White House and, especially, her favorite event of the year: the Kennedy Center Honors, a black-tie extravaganza, always attended by the president and first lady, celebrating the lifetime achievements of major figures in the performing arts.

With her warm personality, genuine interest in other people and keen mind, Sally was a favorite in Washington and immensely popular in Missouri. I have no doubt that many of the invitations we received were intended more for her than for me. Blessed with a remarkable memory, she regularly inquired about people's families, recalling from long-ago conversations the names of their children. In addition to being a loving wife and mother, she was a great political asset.

And Sally had two qualities that stood her well in the serious world of Washington: a sense of the ridiculous and the ability to see the humor in her own life and in mine. A favorite story of hers concerned the wardrobe advice she gave Elizabeth Taylor, then the wife of Virginia senator John Warner. It happened a few days before what was then an annual retreat for Senate Republicans and their spouses, the Tidewater Conference, held at the Tidewater Inn on Maryland's Eastern Shore. Sally, who had grown up star-struck by Elizabeth Taylor's performance in *National Velvet* and had admired the actress's work ever since childhood, was as-tounded, virtually rendered speechless, to receive a phone call from the great lady asking, of all things, what she should wear to the re-treat. Flattered to a degree she had never imagined, Sally, who has an eye for fashion, was honored to give the star the wisdom of her experience. Friday night, Sally said, the women would be casually dressed, wearing pants and a nice blouse or sweater. Saturday night would be dressier, with the women wearing cocktail suits consist-ing of jackets and skirts. Elizabeth Taylor cordially thanked Sally. Immediately on hanging up the phone, Sally called her mother: "You won't believe who just called me and asked *me* what to wear."

We drove to the retreat, where on Friday night the couples gathered for cocktails, the women wearing, as expected, pants and decorative sweaters. Then Elizabeth Taylor made a dramatic en-trance wearing a white caftan and white turban. The next night she wore a purple caftan and purple turban. Sally concludes her story, "So much for my fashion advice."

To be honest, I do not know what a caftan is, but that is not relevant to my relating Sally's story. I tell it only because Sally of-ten tells it on herself. Her readiness to portray herself in human and funny ways endears her to people who know her. As does her readiness to portray me in human and funny ways. To people who call me Senator, she almost always says, "His name is Jack." To someone who asks how often I preach, she is likely to respond, "To me, about five times a day." She has seen it as her mission to disabuse people of a public perception that she thinks is absolutely wrong: that I am a sanctimonious, holier-than-thou Saint Jack.

To acquaintances, to our children and to me, Sally's consistent theme is that she is a down-to-earth person, and we are a down-to-earth family. This is not a contrived message. It is how Sally sees us, and it is how we see ourselves. We are proud of our family, but it is not a boastful or arrogant pride. It is the kind of pride that carries with it responsibility. As D.D. said about not doing drugs, "I knew it was wrong because I'm a Danforth. Peer pressure meant nothing to me."

For our fourth daughter, Jody, being a member of our family carried with it an obligation to do some things out of a sense of duty, whether she wanted to do them or not. She recalls the annual Jefferson City Christmas Parade, when state officers were expected to ride with their families in open convertibles, often in bitter cold. For our children, it was an embarrassment because their schoolmates lined the parade route. One year, Jody remembers, our family had a stomach virus on the day of the parade. She recalls her feelings at the time: "Suck it up; this is your duty."

But for some of our children, there were times when the prominence of family challenged their beliefs in their individual identities. Two daughters questioned whether their applications to colleges had been accepted because of their own merits or because of their family's reputation. Eleanor has told me that she chose the University of Virginia over Princeton and Yale in order to "get lost in the crowd," and that she wanted to get married at a young age so she could change her name. Tom has said that in choosing St.

Olaf College in Northfield, Minnesota, he thought he would be escaping the dominance of family. The strategy did not work because, it turned out, Mel George, then the president of St. Olaf, had arrived there from the University of Missouri.

For Sally, and for at least some of our children, their sense of personal identity was undermined by the nature of my work or by the prominence of the family name. Certainly, this is not what I intended, and I believe it had more to do with the circumstances of being a public family than with me. Indeed, Sally and our children know that, in my heart, they came before politics. But regardless of my intentions, the feeling was there in my family, and it may be there in all political families. It is important to acknowledge the worth of each person. Spouses and children are not satellites of politicians.

The relationship of faith and politics is not about fashioning religious beliefs into political platforms. It is, instead, the way in which faithful people go about the work of politics. If it were the former, family values could be reduced to legislation, but despite the efforts of Christian conservatives, that is not possible. Family values concern how a person, in my case a political person, values his family, his wife and his children. Is the family, especially the spouse, first on the list of priorities, or is it somewhere down the line?

How a politician answers that question tells us a lot about how he does his job. If, to use the phrase my daughter Eleanor heard at her Girl Scout's outing, the politician thinks he is "so great" because of the position he holds, he will be more puffed up with certainty and more uncompromising in his opinions. At the same time, he will be less likely to be a statesman, because a statesman must be willing to leave his office and return home. And he will refrain from taking stands that might cost him that which makes his life meaningful: his job.

Valuing family more than job gives perspectives to politics. It puts the politician in the proper place, which is somewhere less than being the self-perceived agent of God.

If family comes first, the politician needs to find ways to make that clear—by words, symbols and actions. The politician must make the effort. By its nature, the job will not do it for him.

MOVING FORWARD TOGETHER

*C*hristians can have a profound effect on politics without espousing the wedge issues that drive Americans apart. The alternative to the activism of the Christian Right is not passivity, but a different kind of activism, one that emphasizes the reconciling quality of religion as opposed to its divisive force. Such an approach does not preclude taking specific positions on controversial issues; indeed, it is difficult to imagine being engaged in politics without being specific. Nor does this approach preclude championing positions in direct opposition to those taken by the Christian Right. I certainly do, notably by favoring early stage stem cell research. But before Christians, on the Right or the Left, focus on the specifics of a political platform, their challenge is to develop an approach to politics that encourages all Americans to move forward together as one nation.

What follows in this book are some thoughts about how Christians might be constructive participants in America's political life. The starting point is for Christian churches, Christian politicians and Christian citizens consciously to adopt as their own the ministry of reconciliation. I suggest that, in politics, such a ministry would entail a new emphasis on bipartisan problem solving and a reconstitution of America's political center. This would mean a de-emphasis of the sharply defined party-line positions that may be useful in campaign commercials, but create stalemate in government.

I then discuss three broad areas where Christians across the political spectrum might find common ground. One such area is peacemaking, where followers of the Prince of Peace, whether liberal or conservative, might find opportunities to mediate the religious components of violent conflict in parts of the world where people kill each other in the name of God. A second broad area of agreement is the commitment of liberal and conservative Christians to show compassion to suffering people simply because those in need are children of God. It is the kind of compassion I witnessed in Sudan, where many varieties of Christians have joined in a common mission to help desperate people. Third, politics involves more than issues. It involves human beings who, whatever their position on questions of public policy, deserve our respect if not our agreement. When politics devolves into character assassination, all Christians should speak out against personal destruction. We may never agree on the issues, but we should all agree that in America, the pursuit of a political cause does not warrant the intentional destruction of a fellow human.

I conclude the book with a discussion of a chapter in the Bible that has special meaning to me as I think about faith and politics: the twelfth chapter of the Letter to the Romans. It is Paul's advice to first-century Christians in Rome and, I think, to Christians today who want to be faithful workers in the world of politics. Far from being an agenda, it is only an approach to politics, but I think it is an approach that makes it possible for Americans of very different politics to move forward together.

What follows are only one person's thoughts about being a faithful Christian in politics. You will have your own ideas. No doubt, there are many ways for us to be reconcilers.

THE NEED TO
SPEAK OUT AND TO ACT

P rompted by the extraordinary intervention of Republican officeholders in the case of Terri Schiavo, I wrote two opinion columns in 2005 that were published by the *New York Times*, both on the same general subject—one from the perspective of politics, the other from the perspective of religion. The first column expressed alarm that conservative Christians had taken over the Republican Party. The second argued that Christians who are moderate in their politics should be more vocal in expressing a faith-centered alternative to the agenda of their conservative brethren, an alternative based on the Love Commandment. Since the publication of those two columns, I have restated the same views in a number of public appearances and media interviews, my purpose being to evoke a reaction and not just to hear the sound of my own voice.

The common response of Christian conservatives has been that I am trying to muzzle them, that beyond disagreeing with their opinions, I am trying to stop them from expressing themselves. Rush Limbaugh, for example, has characterized my position as being "that Christian conservatives need to get out of politics." That characterization is not correct. I have never said such a thing, and I do not believe such a thing. In America, everyone has the right to participate in politics, and many Christians—conservatives, liberals and people in between, including myself—believe we have a religious obligation to do so.

I encourage all Christians, including conservatives, to participate in politics. The more people who express themselves and become politically active, the healthier our democracy. Christian conservatives bring to politics a concern for moral values that is an important contribution to our nation's discourse. Their voices should be heard, and their opinions are entitled to respect. My hope is that participating Christians will cover a broad range of the political spectrum. I want Christians who are politically liberal and moderate as well as conservative to find their voices. Christianity is broad enough to hold within itself a variety of differing opinions.

Good Christians can be liberal, and good Christians can be conservative. A church that practices reconciliation must be inclusive enough to welcome both. But today's conservative Christians do not practice reconciliation. They are combative, and they are divisive. So, I believe, it is important for Christians across the political spectrum to recommit themselves to the ministry of reconciliation, and to do so in words and actions.

Plenty of devout people disagree with both the theology and the politics of Christian conservatives, but they have been strangely silent in expressing themselves. In the public square, Christianity has been identified more with wedge issues than with the implications of the Love Commandment, and that has created the impression that our faith is hard edged and confrontational. Pat Robertson and James Dobson have become widely quoted media personalities while Christians of differing views languish in obscurity.

Within the Republican Party, there has been little resistance to its identification with conservative Christianity. Indeed, many Republicans have welcomed this new source of electoral strength. At the same time, one public opinion poll after another shows that the American people are concerned about our country. They say that America is on the wrong course. They disapprove of both the president and Congress. They do not trust Republicans or Democrats to solve the nation's problems. They know that terrorists are loose in the world, that the budget is out of control, that key social programs cannot be sustained for future generations, that America depends on energy sources from the Middle East and that we cannot afford the growing cost of health care. And they see politicians forever positioning themselves for the next election, never more than two years away, and avoiding important issues while they "energize the base" on abortion and gay marriage.

The most important question in our national life is not whether activists will enact or defeat religious agendas, but whether there is any common ground for agreement on subjects critical to America's future. Finding such common ground was difficult enough in the more collegial times of a decade or so ago. In 1994, the last bipartisan commission on the reform of Social Security and Medicare failed to agree on any measure to save these two social welfare systems, even though an overwhelming majority of the commission said that Social Security and Medicare faced bankruptcy. Suggested remedies were too sharply contested along partisan lines.

That was a decade before the ascendancy of the Christian Right in our nation's politics, with its strategy of dividing Americans by the use of wedge issues. Now that challenge of reaching consensus on difficult subjects is even more daunting. Now the creation of sharp divisions is more than an attribute of party politics, it is the essence of "Christian politics."

Avoiding critical issues may be comfortable and even popular for a time. I have spoken to audiences that refuse to believe overwhelming evidence that Social Security and Medicare are in peril. Many people would rather not think about budget deficits and energy vulnerability. They do not want to make sacrifices unless the emergency is immediate, preferring to let future generations face these problems. Politicians, attuned to the mood of the voters, do not want to cast controversial votes without public support. The will to act on critical issues is lacking, and the hot-button social issues are diversions. But they are not harmless diversions, because their effect is to drive us even further apart when we should be pulling ourselves together.

Christian conservatives have every right to participate in politics, but in their emphasis on wedge issues, they have deliberately created such political hostility that agreement on other issues is even more difficult. It is important for advocates of an alternative view of faith and politics, the ministry of reconciliation, to be more outspoken and more effective. What follows are some ideas on how they might do this, as church people, as politicians and as citizens.

THE CHURCH AND RECONCILIATION

The Church should decide what it wants to be, a reconciling or a divisive force in America. What do I mean by "the Church?" I mean every level of Christendom. I mean ecumenical gatherings, denominations of all sizes, hierarchies, conventions, dioceses, independent churches and parishes. I mean two or three gathered together in Christ's name. I mean each one of us, individually, who has been baptized. Before deciding the question, we should discuss it. What do we think about the Church in the world today? Is it being faithful to the Great Commission in Matthew 28:19 where the risen Lord says we must "make disciples of all nations, baptizing them in the name of the Father and of the Son and of the Holy Spirit, and teaching them to obey everything that I have commanded you"? Indeed, what is the meaning of the Great Commission? Should we proselytize the unwilling, or should we embrace them? Do we agree or disagree with the way in which the Christian Right carries the faith into American politics? Why?

The readiness of Republican politicians to adopt the agenda of Christian conservatives is evidence that the Church has not done a good job of raising and debating the role of religion in politics. Politicians are always eager to pick up supporters where they can, but usually not at the risk of losing even more voters by doing so. It is telling that Republicans have shown little caution in adopting a religious agenda. It suggests a calculation by Republicans that there is little risk in sectarian politics. Virtually all of the pressure has come from one side, which has been vocal and well organized. Conservative Christians have successfully portrayed themselves as "people of faith," as though their opposition comes only from godless heathens. Recently, a Southern Baptist publication in Missouri called wedge issue opponents "pagan." If religious people who do not agree with the conservatives were to make the case that the Christian Right does not speak for them, it is doubtful that politicians would choose one group of believers over another. Christians who do not accept the conservative agenda have not adequately raised the question of the appropriate role of religion in politics. They have given the conservatives free rein. It is important to raise the question to a very visible level to clarify the issue and to engage in a very public debate. Is the Church a reconciling or a divisive force in America and in the world?

Of course, it's much easier to suggest a national debate on faith and politics than to conduct one. That would take a widespread effort involving the commitment and the energy of a lot of people. Church leaders would need to focus the attention of their denominations; pastors would need to preach sermons and organize forums. Church members would need to write letters to editors and communicate their concerns to politicians. Many people would have to proceed on many fronts. Above all, the effort would have to be persistent. It would accomplish little if it was a momentary flash in the pan. It would take a concerted effort to make it clear that a real debate is taking place, that there is more than one way for Christians to engage in politics, that the ministry of reconciliation is an alternative to divisiveness.

I believe that if the choice is clearly presented, most Christians would recognize the dangers of divisive religion in politics, and they would choose the ministry of reconciliation. But that choice would be far from unanimous. Many Christians would argue that, in religion, there is a clear distinction between truth and falsehood. They would say God's truth is certain, and that they know what it is. They would add that it is their duty to advance God's truth through government. As Richard Land of the Southern Baptist Convention recently put it, "We do believe God has a side, that he is not a moderate or relativist on everything." That is a succinct statement of one position in what should be the national debate.

Other Christians would be disinclined to join a debate about faith and politics on either side. They are interested in neither the political agenda of conservative Christians nor the ministry of reconciliation of more moderate Christians. However sharp the differences, conservatives and moderates agree that their faith directs them outward, toward the world around them, and particularly toward the world of politics. In very different ways, conservatives and moderates want to influence public policy, either its content or the way in which it is made. But many Christians would rather turn inward toward their own denominations or parish churches. Their favorite brand of politics is church politics. Or they would rather turn inward toward the condition of their own souls.

The denomination to which I belong, the Episcopal Church, historically has taken upon itself the ministry of reconciliation. Since the sixteenth century, it has seen itself as the *via media*, the middle way between Roman Catholicism and Protestantism. It believes that it has maintained an unbroken connection with the earliest Church, while encompassing the theology of the Reformation. Its members span a range of political, social and theological opinions, but they are united by a common liturgy, and they share the same bread and wine at the same altars. By its tradition and its practices, it is positioned to be a reconciling force in twenty-first-century America. But most press accounts of the Episcopal Church have nothing to do with the ministry of reconciliation. It is as though such a subject were of no interest. The preoccupation of the Episcopal Church has been the propriety of ordaining gay clergy, most notably the openly gay bishop of New Hampshire. Suicide bombers blow up market places in various countries. Our own government is paralyzed by partisanship. And the historically reconciling Episcopal Church has riveted its attention on the bishop of one of the smallest states in the union.

Rather than turning outward to the world, many Christians would prefer to argue among themselves. This is true in parishes as well as denominations. My friend the Reverend Loren Mead, founder of the Alban Institute, once told me, "There's no fight like a church fight." No doubt about it. Church fights can make the meanest political campaigns seem like beanbag. I have seen some of these fights—parish halls filled with red-in-the-face Christians arguing over items in the church budget, angry camps of parishioners arrayed against each other on whether to oust or keep the pastor, and the threats: "I'm never going to give this church another dime." "I'm leaving."

My own theory is that many people engage in church fights because they enjoy them, they find them invigorating, or fighting gives them a sense of importance. Some of the most aggressive church warriors I have known are retirees. It is presumptuous to speculate what is in their minds, but I have wondered whether they find church fights more stimulating than playing cards.

In peaceful churches as well, there are hosts of people who are content to turn inward. They are interested in what goes on within the walls of the building they visit on Sundays. They are inspired by good preaching or moved by good music. Or they are there simply to deepen their own spiritual lives, to care for their own souls. For them, the Church is not political. Many think it should not be political. They do not want to hear politics from the pulpit.

So a debate on faith and politics, a debate on whether the Church is a reconciling or a divisive force in the world, is something in which they would rather not participate.

On the other hand, their Lord did not tell his disciples to stay at home and take care of themselves. He did not tell them to sit comfortably in their pews and listen to good sermons and sing good hymns. He told them to do something. He sent them into the world to transform the world. How to do this in today's world is the subject for debate. Do we go into the world confident that our truth is, indeed, God's truth, with the idea of implementing that truth through legislation? That is the approach of Christian conservatives. Or is our approach more humble, one that believes that God's truth is larger than anything we could ever contrive? Do we believe that our principal task is not to get our own way, but to advance God's kingdom as best we can while holding together a fracturing world? If that is where we think the Church should be heading, we need to set a course to get us there.

A ministry of reconciliation would have at least these three elements: thinking, speaking and acting. Thinking means establishing a sound theological basis for a reconciling Church. Christians who carry the Gospel into the world should understand the Gospel. Most of us are reasonably nice people who practice tolerance and want to live in a peaceful world, but the same is true for most non-Christians. Merely being nice people falls short of being a ministry of reconciliation. Niceness is a matter of disposition. It lacks the focus and energy of faith. It lacks the commitment to reconciliation when we do not feel like being nice. Christians who are committed to a ministry of reconciliation should have every bit as much focus and energy as conservative Christians who support legislation and back candidates. Their commitment must come from something other than personal disposition. It must come from their understanding of what it means to be a Christian.

I am suggesting rigorous theological analysis of the relationship of faith to politics—something much more than championing one political philosophy or another or one agenda or another. Our best minds should consider how Christians engage in politics and the degree to which we can claim God's truth as our own. Most important, I think they should consider the ministry of reconciliation, how it is rooted in our faith and how it can become the work of the Church. We need a latter-day Reinhold Niebuhr—hopefully, a generation of Reinhold Niebuhrs—who will think about these things and cause the Church to think about them.

Rigorous analysis should take place within the theological seminaries, but it should not remain within the seminaries. If the ministry of the Church is reconciliation, the basis of that ministry must be understood in neighborhood churches by practicing Christians. That means that education and study must be present at the local level, which means educational material, forums and sermons in the churches.

A church that emphasizes a ministry of reconciliation must speak as well as think, addressing its message to people beyond its own walls. It should be at least as outspoken as the divisive church, speaking from its own pulpits, in public forums and through press releases, and it should be persistent, staying on message. A good example of a reconciling church speaking out occurred in my home town in the early 1990s. A pair of radio "shock jocks" had attempted to boost drive-time ratings by including in their repertoire racial and ethnic slurs. Responding to this hatefulness, and understanding its divisive effect on our community, the then Episcopal bishop of Missouri, Hays Rockwell, and the then Catholic auxiliary bishop,

Edward O'Donnell, organized in a matter of hours a very well-covered interfaith media conference to speak out against the radio program. Their effort, an excellent instance of interfaith cooperation, brought an end to the offensive program and promoted healing in the community.

It is important that when the ministry of reconciliation addresses specific political issues, as it will, it clearly disclaims any exclusive right to translate God's will into its own political opinions.

Its message is humility, but it should state it forcefully. It should insist that God's side may have many sides. It should be a clear voice of tolerance, but it should call to task those who claim too readily that they monopolize God's truth. Criticizing Christian moderates, a conservative said, "pastel is not a color." Prophets of a transcendent God who judges the politics of all of us are not pastel.

At a time of extreme partisanship, when our government seems unable to address the most important issues before our country, the message of reconciliation is especially urgent. It is a prophetic message calling politicians to come together, sufficiently, at least, to get on with the nation's business. It is prophecy in the tradition of Isaiah:

"Comfort, O comfort my people, says your God. Speak tenderly to Jerusalem, and cry to her that her warfare is ended . . ." (Isaiah 40:1–2, Revised Standard Version).

A ministry of reconciliation must think, moving beyond goodwill to its theological basis. It must speak, relentlessly proclaiming its prophetic message to a divided world. And it must do more than think and speak. It must act. It must be the reconciling Church.

As I write this, the Muslim world is in an uproar over a cartoon published in a Danish newspaper depicting the prophet Muhammad. In several countries, mobs have rioted, burning Danish flags and attacking diplomatic missions. Some people have been killed. News commentaries have suggested that the demonstrations are not spontaneous, and that they have been drummed up by opportunistic Islamic radicals and encouraged by several governments anxious to stir up opposition to western democracy. The demonstrations are perhaps cynical. Whatever the cause, the violence is unjustifiable. However, a cartoon that mocks religion is certainly offensive and, in today's volatile atmosphere, inflammatory.

A few Christian leaders, including Rowan Williams, the archbishop of Canterbury, and Archbishop Desmond Tutu, have made statements in response to the uproar, but for the most part, this has been a missed opportunity for a reconciling church. Suppose, without necessarily mentioning the cartoon, Christians had found symbolic ways to demonstrate respect for Islam. Suppose, for example, there had been a very public Christian visit to a mosque. The implied message would have been that those who insult Islam do not speak for Christians.

A reconciling church could develop ways for Christians to respond to acts of bigotry in systematic ways. Every time there is a march by the Ku Klux Klan or a swastika painted on a Jewish building, there could be a counteract of reconciliation within twenty-four hours. The counteract could be led by Christians. It could take the form of a religious service emphasizing tolerance or the physical act of cleaning up signs of desecration. Where political disputes have religious components, as in Sudan, churches could actively engage themselves in seeking resolution to conflicts. In a later chapter, I suggest a church-initiated mediation service. My point here is not to champion one approach or another, but to suggest that Christians who are committed to the ministry of reconciliation could, with sufficient imagination and energy, find ways to put their faith into action.

A minimum requirement of a reconciling church is that it do a better job of healing its own internal divisions. This means eliminating or at least reducing the number of church fights that so many of us enjoy. It also means ecumenical outreach and welcoming outsiders to our altars.

POLITICS AND RECONCILIATION

"Make them vote on it." That is a rallying cry commonly heard in Senate caucuses of the two political parties. As a Republican, I can speak from firsthand knowledge only of my own party, but I have no doubt it is equally common in meetings of the Democrats. The caucuses occur on a regular basis every Tuesday the Senate is in session, during the noon hour, each party gathering in a separate room near the Senate chamber, on the second floor of the Capitol. We called our gatherings the policy lunch. After the meal, the elected leadership would report in turn to the members, beginning with the majority or minority leader and continuing through the assistant leader, the conference chair, the policy chair and the senatorial campaign chair. The reports would relate to the program for the week, and the message would often be the same: an exhortation that members stick together as a party. The leadership argued that the party must have clear positions on the issues, and present clear choices to the electorate. If the members were divided among themselves, we could not present clear party positions.

This clarity was said to be especially important when we believed we were on the popular side of an issue, and the Democrats were on the unpopular side. On subjects such as cutting taxes or passing tough criminal laws, we wanted to differentiate ourselves from the Democrats by making them cast roll call votes so that their unpopular opinions would be matters of public record. I am certain that the Democratic policy lunches were very similar, except that their favorite defining issues would be different.

In 1994, in the last months of my Senate career, I became a pariah among Republicans as our party tried to distinguish itself from the Clinton administration on the issue of crime. The administration was supporting a bill, the Violent Crime Control and Law Enforcement Act of 1994, that included not only penalties for crimes but funding for social programs, like the Ounce of Prevention Council, aimed at directing young people into noncriminal activities. One social program, which some called midnight basketball, supported evening sports leagues through the Local Crime Prevention Block Grant Program. Senate Republicans opposed the Clinton bill as soft-on-crime social engineering, and they advanced a substitute proposal, eliminating the social programs and increasing criminal penalties, including greatly expanding the use of the death penalty. A second, but unspoken, reason for Republican opposition was to deny the Democratic president a legislative victory. The Republican strategy was to filibuster the administration's bill.

I could not go along with the Republican strategy because I did not support the death penalty, and I agreed with some of the proposed social programs, including an educational initiative proposed by Bill Bradley and me. So I agreed to vote for cloture and end the filibuster. The cloture motion succeeded 61 to 38. My Republican colleagues thought I had betrayed them. The clear-line distinction they had planned on the highly political issue of crime was being blurred by a fellow Republican. In a meeting in Senator Dole's office, members of the party leadership ardently tried to persuade me to oppose cloture. When their efforts proved unsuccessful, Pete Domenici, a good Senate friend, said, "Let's go to lunch." Together we walked down the marble stairway to the Senators' Dining Room, really two rooms reserved only for senators, the one closest to the door traditionally occupied by Republicans. As we opened the door, we heard the usual sound of friendly mealtime chatter from perhaps a dozen Republican senators who were enjoying their lunch. Then they noticed me at the door. Then absolute silence. It was as though someone had pushed a mute button. It was worse than eerie. It was devastating. I was at the end of my eighteen years in the Senate, at a time when I had hoped to be borne away by the warm feelings of people I had known so well, and I was getting the cold shoulder. Such is the pressure to stick with the party on defining issues.

Defining political issues, with all Republicans on one side and Democrats on the other, are usually issues at stalemate. Normally, neither party has such overwhelming strength that it can work its will over intense opposition without at least some support from the other side. So clearly defined party-line positions may serve a perceived political end, but they are unlikely to be much help in addressing our nation's problems, such as crime.

In addition to matters of party loyalty, individual senators have their own ideas of defining issues to bring to the floor, and every senator has the right to offer amendments. Jesse Helms of North Carolina was particularly enthusiastic about amending appropriations bills to cut the National Endowment for the Arts to prevent the government from funding artists or writers he considered salacious or offensive. On at least one occasion, he came to the Senate floor with a stack of sexually explicit photographs by Robert Mapplethorpe.

A problem with his amendments was that they were so broadly written that they would have prohibited funding for *Huckleberry Finn*. One evening, I did what Jesse considered the unthinkable. As a member of his own party, I made a motion to table, and thereby kill, one of his amendments on the arts. I remember Jesse's comment to me as he stalked from the floor after my tabling motion was successful: "Thanks a bunch."

The nature of modern politics puts a premium on clearly defined, simply explained issues. Are you tough on crime, or are you soft? Are you for offensive art, or are you against it? On the other side, do you support public school teachers, or do you oppose them? Are you the friend of senior citizens, or their foe? Just answer yes or no, which is the form a senator's vote takes when the issue reaches the Senate floor.

It is politics made to order for television, where the coin of the realm is the twenty-second sound bite. On the network news, a three-minute segment is called in-depth reporting. Soon after I arrived in Washington, consultants met with freshmen Republicans to teach us how to make our points in twenty-second sound bites.

Political campaigns are similar. The essence of the campaign is the thirty-second commercial, which is useful for drawing clear distinctions but little else. "My opponent voted against Social Security twenty-eight times." That, and more, can be packed into thirty seconds. But try to explain the bankruptcy of the system in less than half an hour.

The Need to Speak Out and to Act

One looks with awe at the Lincoln-Douglas debates, when crowds were held transfixed for hours by the candidates. Now the public is disgusted by thirty-second commercials. Virtually all discussion about campaign reform is about campaign *finance* reform, as though the heart of America's problem is that politicians are corrupted by money. I think this emphasis misses the point. The problem of campaigns is format, not finances. The thirty-second commercial has reduced politics to clearly defined, simply understood positions. It is politics with sharp edges. Real campaign reform could not abolish the thirty-second commercial, but it could make room for longer, more thoughtful and, hopefully, more civil political discourse.

Campaign format reform would supplement the thirty-second, primarily negative commercial with more substantive opportunities for discussion. But the thirty-second commercial, the twenty-second sound bite, the clear lines of partisan distinction, and the contrived efforts to make the other party cast embarrassing votes would still be with us. No legislation will succeed in transforming American politics into something it is not. Politics that is intentionally divisive will not go away. However, there is an alternative to the present state of affairs. Politics can do a better job of holding the country together and providing a means of moving forward to address significant challenges. There is an important place for politicians who would rather reconcile differences than exacerbate them.

To a degree, the capacity for reconciliation is a matter of personal style. Some people are better than others at projecting an image of reasonableness even while holding very strong opinions. Ronald Reagan had a clear vision of the course of the country, which on fundamental questions of taxes, spending, international trade and foreign policy was quite controversial. But his personal warmth and good humor softened the hard edges of policy disputes. Related to style is the matter of emphasis, the choices politicians make about subjects to pursue, issues to advance, rhetoric to use. No senator has the time, the staff or the interest to be proficient on every matter that comes before Congress, so every senator sets priorities, often related to committee assignments. I spent eighteen years on the very demanding and highly interesting Senate Finance Committee, so my priorities included tax policy and international trade, subjects within that committee's jurisdiction. Or a senator may find some interests that are unrelated to committee work—in my case, hunger in Cambodia and Africa. Another possibility is for a senator to emphasize the wedge issues: abortion, school prayer and the like. It is one thing to vote on such issues, as all senators must, and to speak to them when asked. It is another matter to seek out these issues, to push them relentlessly, to introduce legislation, to speak often and in impassioned tones. Some senators push the wedge issues, openly appealing to the political base. Others de-emphasize them, preferring to concentrate attention on subjects relating to government such as foreign policy, national defense, education and health care.

Beyond personal style and emphasis, it is useful to develop strategies to advance the politics of reconciliation. I will use examples from my own Senate experience to illustrate two important strategies, which are: First, find a problem and solve it, and second, rebuild the political center.

FIND A PROBLEM AND SOLVE IT

The opposite of creating a wedge issue for the purpose of dividing the country is identifying a real problem and fashioning practical ways to solve it. Instead of posturing and speechifying on highly emotional subjects that offer few prospects for constructive resolution, it is possible to bridge philosophical differences in order to achieve practical results. A good example of bipartisan problem solving is the effort to create and improve the Low-Income Housing Tax Credit (LIHTC).

My hometown of St. Louis had become the national symbol of government's failure to provide housing for low-income families when, in 1972, the St. Louis Housing Authority demolished an infamous high-rise project known as Pruitt-Igoe. In the 1960s, recognizing the failure of public housing built and operated by government, Congress shifted its approach by providing subsidies to the private sector for building housing for the poor. These subsidies included several tax incentives, such as accelerated depreciation and special deductions, which were neither well targeted nor effective, and which Congress repealed in the Tax Reform Act of 1986.

The thrust of the 1986 act was to reduce tax rates significantly while abolishing what some people call loopholes, that is, tax breaks provided by law to encourage certain industries and certain investment behavior. At the same time, Congress realized that absent tax incentives, market forces would not suffice to create low-income housing. Low rental rates would not yield sufficient returns to make investment in such housing attractive. So instead of retaining no incentives for housing, the-then chairman of the Finance Committee, Bob Packwood of Oregon, decided it would be better to replace the old, inefficient provisions with a new approach: the LIHTC. Senator George Mitchell of Maine, a Democratic member of the Finance Committee, pushed through a number of refinements on the Senate floor and in the conference with the House, but the credit still emerged as only a temporary three-year program.

The theory of the tax credit was to give investors in affordable housing an adequate return on their investment through a reduction in their taxes in lieu of higher rents. The problem was that just as previous tax breaks had not worked very well, the LIHTC did not work very well either. Investor interest was so modest that in 1987, the first year of the new program, they claimed only 20 percent of the available credits. That is when George Mitchell, who two years later would become majority leader, and I became interested in seeing what we could do to make the new credit work.

As is the case with most Senate activities, the names of the senators were on the work product, but the creativity and hard work were supplied by staff. In this instance, the two bright and energetic staffers were Tracy Kaye of my office and Bobby Rozen of Senator Mitchell's office. In assembling a staff, my objective was to find people on the same wavelength as I, but light-years ahead of me in talent and knowledge of subject matter. That certainly described Tracy, now a professor of law teaching taxation at Seton Hall Law School. For an extended period of time, she dedicated herself to making the LIHTC work. A lesson for senators who want to accomplish positive results is to find excellent staff and encourage them to take initiative.

The first step toward improving the LIHTC was to determine why it was not working. To find out, we created the Mitchell-Danforth Task Force, comprised of people who were knowledgeable in the field of low-income housing. The task force included developers, representatives of tenant groups, nonprofit organizations, and state agencies as well as academics. Its work resulted in a report recommending a variety of changes in the law that Senator Mitchell and I incorporated into two pieces of legislation enacted by Congress in 1989. The bills were noncontroversial and were cosponsored by a bipartisan coalition of senators.

The creation and reform of the LIHTC is an example of both political parties jointly recognizing a public need—an increase in the supply of affordable housing for low-income people—and blending the ideological contributions of liberals and conservatives. Across the political spectrum, senators realized that without government intervention, the private sector would not meet the needs of the poor. At the same time, liberals and conservatives understood that private investors and developers were better equipped to build, own and operate low-income housing than was the government. Finally, liberals and conservatives saw the desirability of decision making at the state level. Under the LIHTC, developers compete for tax credits on the basis of priorities assessed at the state level. State governments receive an allocation of tax credits from the federal government, and state governments award the credits.

As a result of bipartisan identification of a problem and bipartisan creation of a solution, the LIHTC works. Through 2004, it had produced 1.7 million low-income housing units. A knowledgeable person recently told me that the LIHTC is responsible for nearly all low-income housing currently produced in the United States.

The successful bipartisan work to improve the LIHTC is striking in light of a remark I recently heard from a St. Louis friend,

Martie Aboussie. Martie has spent most of his life in Democratic politics in the City of St. Louis. He was alderman and his party's committeeman for the Ninth Ward, on the city's south side. He became a senior member of the Board of Aldermen, and later served as director of the city's Department of Public Safety. In 2001, he retired from public office where, for decades, he had put his stamp on the most important issues before city government, and he devoted himself to good works for the poor. He is executive director of Father Dempsey's Charities, a St. Louis archdiocesan organization that provides transitional housing, food and social services to displaced persons in St. Louis.

Martie is a devout Roman Catholic whose home equally comprises devotional objects and baseball memorabilia. He is one of God's good people, and he is especially worried about how budget cuts, particularly cuts in Medicaid, affect people in need. The words he used in discussing this with me caught my attention. He said, "Republicans are mean, and Democrats are silly." In his opinion, either through callousness or ineptitude, neither party is doing an adequate job of helping those who need help the most.

Helping the poor is clearly a religious value. People sift through scripture, searching for passages to support one wedge issue or another. They find a passage here to support the notion that life begins even before conception. They find a passage there that condemns gays. They advocate school curriculums based on the first chapter of Genesis. No such sifting is required to discover what the Bible says about the poor.

In *God's Politics*, Jim Wallis describes how, as a young man, he and other first-year seminary students searched the Bible for references to the poor: "We found *several thousand* verses in the Bible on the poor and God's response to injustice. We found it to be the second most prominent theme in the Hebrew Scriptures (Old Testament)—the first was idolatry, and the two often were related. One of every sixteen verses in the New Testament is about the poor or the subject of money (Mammon, as the gospels call it). In the first three (Synoptic) gospels it is one out of ten verses, and in the book of Luke, it is one in seven!"

From the blistering condemnation of those who "trample on the poor" and "lie on beds of ivory" in the Book of Amos to Jesus's consignment of those who do not feed the hungry and clothe the naked to eternal punishment in Matthew, both Old and New Testaments are consistent in their message. Mistreatment of the poor is a grievous sin. So is ignoring them. The Gospel of Luke (16:19–31) contains the story of a rich man who "was dressed in purple and fine linen and feasted sumptuously every day" while at his gate a poor man named Lazarus "longed to satisfy his hunger with what fell from the rich man's table." After the rich man's death, he suffered the agony of hell, not for any specific misdeed to Lazarus, but for letting the poor man remain at his gate while he lived sumptuously.

Republicans and Democrats will disagree about how to help the poor. The reform of the LIHTC showed that when the two parties focus on problem solving, they can achieve positive results. There is no excuse for meanness. There is no excuse for silliness.

REBUILD THE POLITICAL CENTER

Every few months, David Boren of Oklahoma asked me the same question, "Why don't we start our own party?" I never took it seriously, never believing David intended it that way. We both understood that America has a two-party system, and I thought, and assumed that he thought, that it would remain that way. Two parties have been good for America, as each has spanned a range of political philosophy, each having a significant number of members who are liberal and a significant number who are conservative, although the center of gravity of each is certainly different. I believed that the range of opinion within it had a moderating effect on each party, and a moderating effect on American politics. I thought this was good. Elections in which one party was swept out of power would not swing America wildly from one extreme to another.

David Boren resigned from the Senate in 1994, just before my retirement, to become president of the University of Oklahoma. Even at that time, he was conservative by the standards of Senate Democrats, often voting similarly to moderate Republicans. We knew each other well, and were social as well as Senate friends. We served together on the Finance Committee, so our interests in issues were similar. Our staffs worked closely together on legislative initiatives.

That David asked the same question so often, even if his suggestion was not serious, demonstrated his concern about the state of politics at the time. In his opinion, the Democratic Party was to the Left of him, and the Republican Party was to the Right of me. The best place for American politics was in the center. In our dream world, that is where it would be.

That was in the 1980s and early 1990s, before the more recent shift of the two parties even more sharply toward their polar extremes. Then, at least, there were enough moderate Republicans in the Senate to elect John Chafee of Rhode Island to the third highest position in our party's leadership, and moderates such as

Lloyd Bentsen of Texas were influential among Senate Democrats. Now the collapse of the political center, sufficiently well along to warrant the repeated comments of David Boren fifteen years ago, has advanced to the point where it is a teetering ruin of its former strength.

Many people, especially those on the ideological extremes, welcome the collapse of the center as a positive development in American democracy. They believe that the American people deserve clear choices when they go to the polls, choices between distinct political ideologies. They think that their party, whichever it is, should portray itself in vivid philosophical colors, in sharp contrast to the opposition. They agree with the slogan of Barry Goldwater's 1964 presidential campaign. In their view, the American people deserve "a choice not an echo." For believers in clear choices of political direction, the twenty-second sound bite and the thirty-second commercial present no problem whatever. Simplicity of message is the goal, and it is well served by using few words. Do not complicate a simple message.

Those who espouse the politics of sharp contrasts despise the political center. In their opinion, the center stands for nothing. It is weak. It is mush. They say, "Pastel is not a color." The daily voice of triumphant conservatism over mealymouthed moderation is Rush Limbaugh.

The alternatives of Right and Left are squarely before the public. They are the platforms of the political parties, the messages of candidates, the two sides presented by television talking heads. They are *Hannity & Colmes*. And these two clearly, strongly, persistently presented alternatives, so dominant that they crowd out all else, raise obvious questions: Is that it? Are those the only choices? Must we be forced to select between extremes?

The reason many American are turned off to politics is not, as party ideologues lament, that they do not have clear enough choices between candidates. It is the opposite. They have extremely clear choices, but they do not like either of them. They do not like either candidate. They do not like either party. I have heard many people use essentially the same words in describing their election-day frustration: "I want to check a box that says, 'None of the above.'"

The frustration many people feel about current political choices is understandable. They realize the major challenges that face our country: terrorism, Medicare and energy, to name a few, and they think that instead of making serious progress, we are bogged down by the state of our politics. They sense that what is truly weak in American politics is not what remains of the center. What is weak is the partisanship of the extremes.

Ideologues claim that centrists stand for nothing. The ideologues stand for a lot. They have reduced it to emotionally charged sound bites. But they accomplish nothing, and they can accomplish nothing. They are all talk and no do. They have led us into stalemate.

The framers of our Constitution designed our government to be slow moving, with three branches and two houses of Congress. The right of unlimited debate in the Senate allows one strongly held position to block action by another. The Senate is indeed a deliberative body, and that quality serves the nation well. A slow-moving government helps us maintain a stable government. But slow moving is not the same as immobile. Motion occurs when there is a convergence of competing ideas, somewhere in the center. Without convergence, without the center, there is stalemate.

A political strategy that sets out extreme positions, leaving no room for compromise with the opposition, may succeed in winning elections; but if there is no basis for progress when the election is over, it is hard to justify winning. Yes, the victor may have a title such as senator or congressman, and an office and a staff. But to what end? What happens next? The work of government must be more than issuing press releases.

Ideologues claim that the center is mush. But real mush is where there is a lot of talk and no action. Strength results in action, and the center is where the action is. It is important to rebuild America's political center. The Civil Rights Act of 1991 is an example of how to do that.

The history of the 1991 act begins two years earlier when the Supreme Court decided a number of cases that limited the ability of aggrieved parties to enforce civil rights laws relating to discrimination in employment. The most significant of those cases was *Wards Cove Packing Co. v. Atonio*, which made it more difficult for plaintiffs to prove discrimination in "disparate impact cases," that is, cases involving employment standards which, while not discriminatory on their face, had the effect of screening out minorities or women. Examples in the case law of disparate impact are height and weight standards for law enforcement officers (disproportionately screening out women) and the requirement that manual laborers have high school diplomas (disproportionately screening out African Americans). The legal debate has been about when requirements that screen out minorities are permissible under the civil rights laws. The issue in *Wards Cove* was how closely an employment standard that screened out minorities had to relate to the performance of the job in question.

Prior to 1989, civil rights groups had looked to the federal courts to advance their cause. Now the courts had dealt them a series of blows, so the groups turned to Congress to overrule the Supreme Court decisions, first approaching their leading champion in the Senate, Ted Kennedy, then asking Peter Leibold, of my staff, whether we could help provide Republican support.

On the recommendation of my daughter Mary, I had hired Pete and his wife, Elizabeth McCloskey, a year earlier, after he had completed a clerkship with a federal appellate court judge. Before their marriage, Mary had shared a New Haven apartment with Liz, who was a student at Yale Divinity School. Pete and Mary were friends and classmates at Yale Law School. Liz and Pete were outstanding additions to my office.

By meeting with Peter Leibold, leaders of the civil rights groups could not have been dealing with a better person. Their subject matter was part of his portfolio within my office, but beyond that, he had just the right skills and character traits for the task at hand. He is very smart, very creative and trained in the law. He has a cheerful personality and a quick sense of humor that help him negotiate hard issues with difficult people. Most important, he and Liz share an idealism and commitment to good causes firmly rooted in their Catholic faith.

Just west of the Russell Senate Office Building, where my Senate office was located, is a pleasant park, at the center of which is a carillon dedicated to the memory of Senator Robert A. Taft. It is an excellent place for walking and for thinking. During a midday walk in that park, Pete and I discussed the state of the civil rights law, the recent Supreme Court decisions, the ideas of Senator Kennedy and the concerns of President George H. W. Bush's administration. Pete said that it was important to correct the problems created by the Supreme Court's decisions, but that the administration was opposed to any legislation that would create incentives for employers to use numerical quotas for employment. He suggested that there were wording changes that could be made in Senator Kennedy's bill that would satisfactorily address the administration's concerns that the bill would result in employers resorting to quotas to avoid liability. Finally, with his characteristic enthusiasm, Pete described the role I could play in enacting legislation. He said that the only possibility of correcting the Supreme Court's decisions was in the political center, that the civil rights groups would not be able to pass a bill that accomplished all their wishes, and that some conservatives would resist any legislation. He said that I should take the centrist position and help get a bill passed.

Pete convinced me. I authorized him to work with Senator Kennedy's staff to create a bill that could win the support of at least some Republican senators. He negotiated those changes, which were resisted by the civil rights groups, but which, we believed, made the legislation less susceptible to the label "quota bill." The result would have been the Civil Rights Act of 1990, which passed the Senate by a vote of 62 to 34, with the support of nine Republican senators, but it was vetoed by President Bush. The Senate failed to override the veto by a single vote, so Senator Kennedy's effort, the Civil Rights Act of 1990, was dead.

In May 1991, I told Pete that we would renew the effort to enact a civil rights law, this time with only Republican cosponsors. Two important ideas were in my mind. First, the decisions of the Supreme Court had to be undone. The Court had steered America in the wrong direction. The nation had turned backward in civil rights, and that was something we should not do. In providing equal opportunity, America's course should be forward, and only forward. Moreover, we should make every effort to extricate what should be a national commitment to civil rights from the extremely divisive question of quotas.

Second, I agreed with Pete that the only solution to the civil rights problem was in the political center, and I thought it important for Republicans to take the lead in building the center. Ours had been, and must continue to be, the party of Lincoln. I was confident that President Bush did not want his veto to stand as his last word on civil rights, so responsibility for correcting problems in the civil rights laws would have to be taken by centrists in the Republican Party.

My strategy was to put together and keep together as large a bloc of like-minded Republican senators as possible, senators who wanted to move forward on civil rights without quotas. In 1991, I also wanted to introduce legislation that addressed an additional concern I had with Senator Kennedy's 1990 bill, which had provided unlimited damages for victims of discrimination under a particular title of the civil rights laws. As a strong believer in tort reform, I did not believe it wise to have uncapped punitive and noneconomic damages in tort law, let alone in civil rights laws. With these substantive and political goals in mind, I set out to recruit Republican senators who wanted our party to be in the political center, and get things done. Even then the center had been taken for granted. Moderates had been marginalized. It was time for us to take the lead.

We began by introducing a package of three bills with nine Republican cosponsors, the most crucial of whom was Warren Rudman of New Hampshire, because he had supplied the one-vote margin to sustain the president's veto in the previous year. In addition to Warren Rudman and me, the nine Republicans included John Chafee of Rhode Island, Bill Cohen of Maine, Pete Domenici of New Mexico, Dave Durenberger of Minnesota, Mark Hatfield of Oregon, Jim Jeffords of Vermont and Arlen Specter of Pennsylvania. The support of these nine senators was crucial because without us, no civil rights bill would pass the Senate, and with us, no presidential veto would withstand an override vote. Our willingness to stand together was crucial, and although the administration persuaded certain senators to drop off as cosponsors of subsequent legislative drafts, I succeeded in obtaining assurances from those same senators that they would ultimately support the legislation on the floor of the Senate. Together with Democrats, we comprised a veto-proof majority, and everyone interested in the legislation knew it: the administration, Senator Kennedy, the civil rights groups and business organizations. Senator Kennedy understood that we would vote for our bill, and only for our bill. The Republican center would be taken seriously.

Seriously, but not always happily—civil rights groups thought we were hijacking their bill; Democrats thought we were going easy on business. The administration persisted in its concern that where there were statistical imbalances, businesses would resort to statistical quotas in order to avoid lawsuits. Throughout the summer, we engaged in extensive negotiations with both sides, carefully wordsmithing the language of the bill. Peter Leibold, then three years out of law school, did the difficult, lawyerly work, negotiating fine points with the president's chief of staff, John Sununu, and White House legal counsel, Boyden Gray. During one negotiating meeting with the White House, Senator Kennedy, waiting outside Senator Dole's capitol office, sent in a note asking if he could speak with me. In the corridor, he asked if I could help him on the issue of caps on damages. The civil rights groups were pressing him. If we could not eliminate the caps, could we at least raise them? No, I responded, I could not help him.

When the negotiations ended, Senator Strom Thurmond, who

in 1948 had been the Dixiecrat candidate for president, asked me to include his name as close to the top of the list of cosponsors as possible. Ted Kennedy stood resolutely on the Senate floor defending the bill and opposing amendments, even those with which he philosophically agreed. He proved himself a man of his word, supporting what he knew was the best deal he could make. Finally, on an overcast autumn day in the White House Rose Garden, President Bush signed the bill into law. After doing so, he rose, stepped around the table, walked to the front row of seats and handed me the signing pen.

I am not sure that, in practice, the Civil Rights Act of 1991 has turned out to be as good as I had hoped at the time. Some people have told me that it has created a lot of work for lawyers, which definitely was not my intention. I am told that the damages available under Title VII, even if capped, may have more to do with de facto quotas than the disparate impact provisions. But if Congress had to err in the area of civil rights, I would rather have the error be in favor of action than inaction. And I would rather have employers redress cases of inequality than not, even if their motivation is fear of litigation.

The key to passing the Civil Rights Act of 1991 was the willingness of nine centrist senators to remain bound together throughout the difficult months of contentious politics. Typical of controversial issues, partisans on each side took extreme positions and used extreme rhetoric to motivate their supporters. At one point, former secretary of transportation William Coleman, representing the civil rights groups, angrily threatened to walk out of my office. People within the administration repeatedly raised the specter of quotas. Through the political storm, nine moderate Republican senators stuck together.

The Need to Speak Out and to Act

Sticking together for an extended period of time is something senators do not do naturally. Senators are independent of each other. Each sees issues differently. Each has different constituents, each has, to at least some degree, pride of authorship. The impulse is to separate and go in different directions.

What nine senators proved in 1991 was that on an important issue, a small number of swing votes can determine the course of legislation, provided that those who cast them have worked together, acted together, and refrained from making separate, individually arranged deals. That is a huge and essential proviso. They must communicate with each other, and they must trust each other. They must see themselves as a bloc. If they adopt a centrist position, and if they stick together, others will gravitate toward them. That is the lesson of the Civil Rights Act of 1991.

In 1991, the Senate had more than nine moderate Republicans from whom to convene the bloc that sponsored the civil rights legislation. Today, the number of moderate Republicans is smaller. That means that, of necessity, the creation of a centrist group might require a bipartisan approach. In 2005, just such a coalition came together to forestall what was called the nuclear option, a proposed change in Senate rules relating to the filibuster of judicial nominees. It consisted of seven Democrats and seven Republicans who pledged that they would stay together, at least on that contentious subject.

Other subjects come to mind where nearly everyone realizes that America has serious problems, but where our polarized parties are unable to act. Entitlement reform and energy policy are obvious candidates. The key is for centrists to see themselves as a group and, one issue at a time, to bind themselves together.

CITIZENS FOR RECONCILIATION—
HOW TO START A MOVEMENT

Many Americans have asked me what they can do to change politics in our country. They believe that something is terribly wrong, that politics is polarized on Left and Right, and that neither the talking heads shouting on television nor most of the candidates speak for them. They want to do something, but they do not know what to do, so many of them are inclined to give up without an effort.

People in my own party have told me that they have always been Republicans, but that the party no longer stands for their beliefs. So, they have said, they are thinking of quitting. My response is always the same: "Please don't do that." Our party is worth saving. The center of American politics is worth rebuilding.

What can we do if we do not agree with today's divisive style of politics that relies on wedge issues? What can we do if we think the Republican Party has become the arm of the Christian Right? What can we do to restore a political center capable of reconciling the polar differences of politics—capable of solving problems, not just winning elections? If those are our concerns, we should not give up. We should speak, and we should act.

When the people speak, politicians listen. A lot of disgruntled people do not believe that. They claim that because government does not do what they want it to do, politicians do not care what they are saying. They are wrong. The business of politics is listening, and then telling people what they want to hear. The old marketing slogan "The customer is always right" applies to winning peoples' votes, just as it applies to winning their business. Politicians listen, but the voices they hear are not from the center. The voices they hear are those of the activists, the people who care enough to show up at town hall meetings and attend rallies, and express themselves on issues. They are citizens with strongly held ideas, and they organize themselves around those ideas. Whether Republicans or Democrats, they are the base.

To change American politics, new voices must make themselves heard by politicians. They must speak for the center and against the extremes; they must speak with urgency about the need for solving problems as opposed to making campaign points. They must emphasize reconciliation and de-emphasize wedge issues.

There are a number of ways people can express themselves to politicians. A simple means is the telephone. They can phone the office of elected officials. Or they can phone into radio talk shows. One afternoon, the late Bob Hardy, host of the *At Your Service* call-in show on KMOX radio in St. Louis announced that the Senate was about to vote to give itself a pay raise. Three hours later, he reported that 170 listeners had phoned in, all of whom opposed Congress raising its pay. Few members of Congress are willing to buck that kind of intense opposition.

E-mail is very effective. So was letter writing until the anthrax scare dramatically slowed down the delivery of mail in the Capitol. Attending public meetings is especially effective in impressing politicians. My Senate office used to mail postcards to entire zip codes announcing the time and place for my next "town hall meeting." Most such meetings were attended by hundreds of people, nearly all of whom were angry about something. I hated those meetings, since I was the lightning rod for anger against government in general or against some position I had taken in the Senate, but I thought it was important to hear from even the angriest of my constituents, and to explain my views to them. The town hall meetings were strong evidence that the people who bother to express themselves are those with intense, and often hostile, opinions.

It is important not just to complain about what you do not like in government but also to support what you do like. Support, too, can come in different forms. It may be a contribution of money to an election campaign, or it may be the commitment of time and energy to a favored candidate. It may be something as simple as an encouraging word. Always, it meant a great deal to me when constituents were kind enough to say, "You're doing a good job."

The fact is that participating in politics is not only important, it is also easy. It is easy to make a phone call, or send an e-mail, or attend a meeting or help a campaign. What is problematic is the motivation to do these easy things, especially on a sustained basis. Politicians are accustomed to brief bursts of attention, even very negative attention. Whatever the problem, they think they can ride it out. "It's a one-day story," they tell themselves, even if the story is a scandal. The public has a short memory, and the term of office for a senator is six years. So it is important for interested citizens to have enough motivation to do more than raise issues. They must be willing to stay with their issues for prolonged periods of time. Such staying power is more characteristic of some citizens than others.

Staying power is characteristic of people who have an economic interest in an issue. Their attention is more than a matter of their political opinion. It is a matter of dollars and cents. Moreover, if they become sidetracked by the normal distractions of life—baseball games and school plays and their favorite television programs—their economic interests make it worthwhile to hire people who will stay on message when they cannot. Such hired representatives are called lobbyists.

Then there is the long-term interest sustained by passion. This is the interest of the true believers, convinced of the justice of the cause and willing to devote time and treasure to its battles. These are people who take wedge issues as their own, who embrace them with devotion. They are people who not only write Congress, they march on Washington. Their commitment to their causes and their willingness to fight for their beliefs make their support a prize worth seeking by politicians. For each party, these true believers make up the political base.

Some moderates have economic motives for their politics, but many do not, and economic motives for sustained political activity are often absent. So, frequently, is their emotional commitment to issues. By temperament, moderates do not share the passionate intensity of the true believers. It is difficult to imagine a centrist fired up enough to use the words made popular in the movie *Network*: "I'm mad as hell, and I'm not going to take it anymore."

If not driven by economic interest or by passion for an ideology, what would motivate a centrist to be active in politics, particularly on a sustained basis? Two answers come immediately to mind. The first is love for country, or perhaps more broadly, love for the world God gave us. It is a desire to live in a just, prosperous and peaceful world and in a country in which we take enormous pride. It is a sense of stewardship, a desire to keep building such a world and such a country, and to pass them on, even better and more secure, to generations that come after us. It is patriotism, the love of country more than self. It is a conviction that we will succeed in building the America and the world we want for our grandchildren only if we start by overcoming our differences and finding our common ground. In our moderation, we claim certainty of very little, but we are certain of this: Practitioners of divisiveness cannot achieve our vision of what America or the world should be. Day by day, they are moving that vision further and further beyond our reach. For the sake of the vision, centrists must speak and act.

The second motive is love of God. It is the knowledge that God has made us for his purpose and has sent us into his world. It is the belief that we must speak and act because God commands us to speak and act. We have a God-given commission, but it is not a commission to be self-righteous know-it-alls—quite the contrary. Our work in God's world begins with the acknowledgment that we are not God, and that our most bitter rivals are made in God's image. That acknowledgment makes it possible for us to do the work God has given us to do: the ministry of reconciliation.

Finally, we are not independent agents, and we cannot be effective if we act as such. People who stand alone on principle are admirable, but in politics, their chances of accomplishing much are slim. This must be a group enterprise, a movement. The more people who are involved, the better. Group enterprises require organization.

Within the Republican Party, at least two estimable moderates have commenced such organizational efforts. Former congressman Amory Houghton, Jr., of New York has founded the Main Street Partnership, described as the largest group of elected Republican moderates in the country, and former governor of New Jersey and former EPA administrator Christine Todd Whitman has started IMP-PAC, or It's My Party Too Political Action Committee. This is a political action committee with the mission of advancing "the issues that help define moderate members of the Republican Party." For a number of years, the Democratic Leadership Council has worked to rebuild the center of its party. These are worthy endeavors, meriting the support and membership of people who want to improve American politics.

The Need to Speak Out and to Act

Beyond political organizations, the concerted efforts of Christians for change can find their locus where believers join together to be the body of Christ, which is the Church. The Church should not embrace particular platforms or endorse candidates or support political parties, for that would create the very divisiveness it is meant to overcome. But the Church can be a persistent voice against such divisiveness, and it can equip its members for the ministry of reconciliation.

BLESSED ARE THE PEACEMAKERS

S udan is a large country on a north-south axis, straddling the fault line between Arab Africa and Black Africa. The north, where the capital, Khartoum, is situated, is predominantly Arab and politically dominant. The government is Islamic. Flying south from Khartoum, one crosses the Nuba Mountains, then the world's largest swamp, the Sudd, which historically has been a geographical barrier separating much of black Sudan from the north. Black Sudanese have long believed that they are second-class citizens, a belief borne out by reality. That belief inspired their armed rebellion against the government. The differences between southern Sudan and the government are complex, involving race, ethnicity and competing claims to oil reserves. Especially, black Sudanese have strongly resisted the government's efforts to impose Arabic language and culture on the whole of the country, efforts that included the teaching of Arabic in schools and compelling blacks to adopt Arab names.

All black Sudanese with whom I spoke resisted the imposition of Islamic law on their people. Religious differences are not the sole cause of conflict between black Sudanese and the government, but they are a component of the conflict. While most, if not all, Arab Sudanese are Muslim, blacks represent various religions. Some are Christian, many of whom are Catholic or Anglican, some are Muslim and some are practitioners of traditional African religions. After President George W. Bush asked me to explore how the United States could advance the prospects for peace in Sudan, it seemed to me that a meeting with religious leaders would be a good place to start. So at my request, Ray Brown, then our chargé d'affaires in Khartoum, arranged a meeting for me with religious leaders at the American embassy there. The meeting turned out to be, if not a disaster, a profound disappointment.

Maybe fifteen Sudanese clergy attended the meeting. Four or five were Muslim, wearing the full white robes and turbans of Sudanese Arabs. The rest were Christian, Catholic, Anglican and one Pentecostal, each in a clerical collar. All seemed reasonably cordial to one another as they arrived in a sparsely appointed room in our decrepit embassy. I opened the meeting by welcoming the guests and thanking them for attending. I told them that President Bush had a keen interest in encouraging peace in their country, and that I was his personal envoy. I explained my understanding that religious differences were partly responsible for the conflict in Sudan, and I said that throughout history, religion had been the cause of bloodshed. However, I continued, many people, including myself, believe that peacemaking should be the mission of all people of faith. I said that, indeed, the meaning of the word "religion" was to bind things together. I expressed hope that religious people of Sudan could work with each other so that instead of being a cause of war, religion could be a means of ending the war and making it possible for all Sudanese to live with each other in peace. I then invited their thoughts, thinking I had made a good little speech and naively expecting the clergy in attendance to join in a chorus of affirmation and pledge cooperation with each other. Only as the meeting progressed did I realize what I should have noticed while I was speaking. As I was being carried away by the persuasiveness of my own words, my guests were staring blankly ahead, either at me or at their feet.

The Muslim clergy were first to respond to my opening remarks, speaking one after another, each with essentially the same message. Sudan is one country, they said. All Sudanese, black and Arab, Christian and Muslim, are equal citizens of their common land. While Muslims live according to Sharia law, those requirements do not apply to Christians, who are free to follow their own beliefs and practices. In short, according to the Muslim clergy at the meeting, religion was not a problem in Sudan. Far from being persecuted, Christians were respected fellow citizens of a united country.

The Christians were no longer staring blankly ahead as they had been while I was speaking. Everything in their facial expressions and body language told me they were seething, ready to erupt in anger. When the last Muslim had spoken, they could contain themselves no longer. One by one, they outdid each other in venting their outrage. They were the persecuted minority of Sudan, and the visitor from America should not think otherwise. The Catholic bishop of Juba said he had been forced out of his diocese. Another Catholic said that the government had confiscated Church property. Anglicans said that the government had taken their cathedral and turned it into a museum. Then, during Holy Week, the government had teargassed the makeshift structure they had converted into their new cathedral, a building I had worshipped in the previous Sunday. They could not get government permission to build churches. They could not even get government permission to repair the roofs of existing churches. Then a Pentecostal minister spoke, young, eloquent, overflowing with rage, condemning the government for its persecution of his church and the black people of Sudan.

Most if not all of the Christian clergy who attended the meeting spoke—all with the same tone of outrage. There was no message of reconciliation, no hope of moving together as one people, no word of love or forgiveness. I sat through the speeches feeling sorry that I had brought the group together, thinking this was one of the worst meetings I had ever attended. When the last Christian had spoken, I thanked the group, and with little more to say, depressed by what I had heard, I showed my guests to the door.

In 1996, the United States withdrew its ambassador from Sudan out of fear for the safety of our personnel, and it has since been represented by a chargé d'affaires, who at the time was Ray Brown. For the evening after my meeting with the clergy, Ray had arranged a reception for me at what had been the ambassador's residence, a dusty compound whose most interesting feature was its population of large, lumbering tortoises that hung out around the swimming pool. The reception was well attended by, among others, the same clergy who had been present at the embassy meeting earlier in the day. To my surprise, each faith group, Muslim and Christian, came up to me separately at the reception, and each said the same thing: "That was a wonderful meeting. Thank you for having it. We had never before heard the other side's message. Until today, we had never met each other." Discouraged as I was by the tone of the meeting, their comments at the reception gave me hope that perhaps some good could come from Muslim-Christian dialogue.

The possibility that there might be mediation of the religious component of Sudan's conflict fascinated me, and prompted me to seek the advice of people far more experienced than I. I met with the then archbishop of Canterbury, Lord George Carey, at Lambeth Palace in London. I visited with the then archbishop, now Cardinal Tauran, foreign minister in the Vatican. On two visits to Rome, I went to the headquarters of the Community of Sant'Egidio, a highly respected Catholic organization with an impressive history of mediating political disputes. In Cairo, I called on the sheik of Al-Azhar, a leading figure in Islam. Several times, I met with Ahmed al Mahdi, a wise and good man who, at that time, was imam of the Ansar sect of Islam in Sudan. From these meetings I developed a specific plan.

The plan was for leading religious figures from outside Sudan to appoint a small panel of mediators who would meet with Sudanese Muslims, Christians and government officials, and attempt to reach agreement on specific points of contention. For example, could Sharia law apply to Muslims but not non-Muslims? How could Khartoum, as the capital of a united country, accommodate non-Muslims on matters such as diet and alcohol without offending Muslims? Could Christians be free to build and repair their churches? The idea was that the mediation panel would have such high-level sponsorship that it would command the respect of the Sudanese. In my mind, the pope, the archbishop of Canterbury, the sheik of Al-Azhar and, perhaps, the grand mufti of Jerusalem would appoint the mediators. The work of the panel would be mediation, that is, a search for common ground that the parties could agree to, and not arbitration, which leads to the imposition of binding results. Because mediation would have been a mechanism by which Muslims and Christians could try to work out differences among themselves, and was not a threat that outsiders would try to dictate solutions, I thought that it offered Muslims and non-Muslims much to gain and nothing to lose.

After briefing President Bush on the plan in an Oval Office meeting, I flew to Khartoum and then presented the idea first to representatives of the government, then to Christian clergy. As expected, the two officials of the government, peace negotiator Ghazi Suleiman and Vice President Ali Uthman Muhammad Taha, took the suggestion under advisement, since they could not give me an immediate answer. But I thought that both meetings were positive. Each listened carefully, and each said that the suggestion would receive due consideration. That was the best response I could hope for from an initial meeting.

The Christian clergy, consisting mostly of the same people who had attended the earlier interfaith meeting, joined me in the living room of the ambassador's residence. It was quickly apparent that they had no interest in the idea I was offering. They were polite, and they thanked me for America's interest in their country, but they did not want to mediate anything with the government of Sudan. They were very clear in their position and repeated their recitation of grievances with the government. The government was the oppressor, and they were the oppressed. The differences between black Sudan and Arab Sudan were beyond reconciliation. They were secessionists, and they wanted out.

As a group, the Christian clergy in Khartoum were the most

angry and intractable people I dealt with in Sudan. John Garang, the leader of the rebel Sudan People's Liberation Movement (SPLM), was a tough negotiator, but he was not a secessionist. His dream was a united Sudan in which he and the SPLM would take a significant role. By contrast, the Christian clergy had given up on the idea of peace. Because they saw no place for themselves in a united Sudan, they had no interest in mediating differences with the government. American Christians who had taken up the cause of Sudan gave me the impression that in adopting a hard line against the government, they were taking their cue from their brethren in the Sudanese clergy. Their interest was in making a moral statement against the government, not in attempting to bridge differences.

While Sudanese Christians eschewed a peaceful resolution to the civil war short of secession, the most impressive voice for peace I heard in Sudan was a Muslim clergyman, Ahmed al-Mahdi. Ahmed is a grandson of the Mahdi, the messianic warrior who drove the British out of Sudan, and he is a deeply spiritual man who honored the rights of non-Muslim minorities, and who wanted to do his part to hold his country together. In my lifetime, I have met two people whose physical appearances have exuded their inner spirituality. They seemed literally aglow with their faith. One was Pope John Paul II, the other was Ahmed al-Mahdi. I often told Ahmed that he was my spiritual brother, but I think that was unduly flattering to me.

I had the privilege of visiting with Ahmed a number of times, once at a dinner he hosted for me in his home overlooking the Nile. It was an impressive gathering of Sudanese, including a former president of the country, and to my western eyes, it was an exotic evening as we feasted on charcoal-grilled lamb with scores if not hundreds of the imam's followers. During the evening, we gathered on the balcony of his home where Ahmed read a speech of welcome. His public message to his coreligionists was what he had said to me in private. He longed for a peaceful Sudan where all people, Arab and black, Muslim and non-Muslim, could live together as equals.

The contrast between Ahmed al-Mahdi, Muslim cleric and grandson of the Mahdi, and the Christian clergy who met with me in the ambassador's residence was striking. The Muslim was the peacemaker. The Christians were the angry secessionists. I do not say this to blame the Christians. Given their persecution by the government, I understand their anger. But my experience belied the stereotypes of peaceful Christians and militant Muslims that many Americans have embraced. Since 9/11, what Americans hear about Islam is a relentless message of violence. Nearly every day the news is the same, bombings of civilians in Iraq or Jordan, riots in France. It is easy to convince ourselves that Islam is a religion of violence, and Christianity is a religion of peace. In Sudan I learned that these stereotypes do not hold.

Before we Christians focus too intently on the speck in our Muslim neighbors' eye, it is well to consider whether there is a log in our own eye. That is, is Christianity as peaceful a religion as we would like to believe? And if it is, are Christians as effective at peacemaking as we should be?

It is natural for us to assume that an emphasis on peace is at the heart of Christianity. Jesus said, "Blessed are the peacemakers." Many Christians greet each other at worship with the words, "the peace of the Lord." A familiar blessing begins, "The peace of God which passes all understanding." We send Christmas cards that proclaim, "Peace." Although most Christians do not think that pacifism is a successful strategy for coping with a dangerous world, we honor its place in Christianity.

On the other hand, Jesus said, "Do not think that I have come to bring peace to the earth; I have not come to bring peace, but a sword" (Matthew 10:34). Sunday School children, who learn that Joshua won the Battle of Jericho, read that immediately after the walls came down, Joshua's army slaughtered "all in the city, both men and women, young and old, oxen, sheep and donkeys" (Joshua 6:21). In the year 1095, Pope Urban II dispatched armies of Crusaders to reclaim the Holy Land from Muslims with the chilling exhortation: "I, or rather the Lord, beseech you as Christ's heralds to publish this everywhere and to persuade all people of whatever rank, foot-soldiers and knights, poor and rich, to carry aid promptly to those Christians and to destroy that vile race from the lands of our friends . . . Christ commands it." In our own time, Christians who take to heart the apocalyptic vision of the book of Revelation look forward to the end of time when the warrior Christ will appear on a white horse to slay the forces of the Antichrist. Believing that the end will come when Israel claims all the land God promised Abraham, they oppose diplomatic initiatives in the Middle East that include giving up Israeli land in Gaza and the West Bank in exchange for peace.

I believe that Christianity is a religion of peace, and that peace, forgiveness and reconciliation are central Gospel themes. But we should not take such a conclusion for granted. Christians in the past and in the present have shown themselves capable of bloodshed in the name of religion, so the assumption that Christianity is a religion of peace has not always been borne out in reality. Also, as is often the case with what we assume to be true, truths that we take for granted escape our attention and lose their ability to affect the way we live. If for Christians, the concept of peace has little more meaning than a word on a Christmas card, then it has insufficient power to be an effective influence in Sudan or anywhere else.

When I was a first-semester law student, a very demanding professor named Grant Gilmore singled me out in contracts class for an exercise in Socratic teaching. I have no memory of the case or the legal principle we were discussing, but I have a vivid recollection of one lesson learned from that classroom exchange. To one of Professor Gilmore's questions, I responded, "I assume that's true." His retort was immediate: "Don't assume anything, Mr. Danforth." I think Christianity is a religion of peace. I want that to be true. But we should assume nothing, for if we merely assume it, we relegate peace to the status of a Christmas card sentiment. In our seminaries, in our churches, in our thoughts and prayers we should give rigorous attention to whether Christianity is a religion of peace. And if it is, we should think about how we can be more effective peacemakers than we have been to date.

This may be unfair, but I have the feeling that many church-sponsored initiatives on peacemaking are what are known as *kumbaya* meetings. People of goodwill gather together to discuss the importance of greater understanding among groups and to pray for peace. This is fine, as far as it goes, but it does not go far enough. If churches want to be effective in peacemaking, it is important to do more than rely on goodwill. It is important to develop strategies likely to accomplish real results. One such strategy might be the kind of conflict-specific mediation service I attempted to promote in Sudan.

In 2004, while serving as America's representative to the United Nations, I tested the idea of creating a mediation service that could be permanently available to help resolve religious components of political conflicts. The proposal was for the Security Council to create a panel of mediators that it could draw upon to help resolve conflicts in places like Sudan, where religion is part of the problem. Under the United Nations Charter, the prevention and resolution of conflict is a responsibility of the Security Council, so it seemed that the council was the place to house such a facility. Some within the State Department resisted the idea, questioning whether the Security Council should wade into controversial questions of religion, but Secretary Colin Powell authorized me to test the idea with representatives of other countries. I did so, receiving a range of responses. The Philippines, which had circulated a draft resolution on religious conflict of its own during the most recent meeting of the General Assembly, was especially enthusiastic, and joined immediately as our partner in advancing the idea. Other countries, including China, were skeptical or cool. After devoting a significant amount of time discussing the concept with fellow delegates, I concluded that their response was not sufficiently positive to provide any real hope that the Security Council would adopt the proposal, at least in the foreseeable future.

But although the Security Council would be the obvious sponsor of an entity existing for the purpose of maintaining peace, council sponsorship is not the only possibility. The same result can be achieved by a different approach. Even if a mediation service would exist outside the United Nations and under some different auspices, it could, nevertheless, be available to the Security Council or the Secretary-General as a resource for addressing religious conflict. Its work could be done by a very small staff that could be independent of the United Nations Secretariat. A key to its success would be its credibility, which would be established if it is created by world religious leaders, and if it combines recognized expertise both in the subject matter of religion (where most statesmen have no expertise) and in the techniques of dispute resolution.

The notion that religious leaders and groups should move beyond *kumbaya* gatherings and develop results-oriented methods to address religious conflict has been pursued by others. In October 2005, Franciscans International convened a meeting in Washington, D.C., to consider ways in which religious groups might engage in practical peacemaking initiatives. A month later, the Reverend Samuel Kobia, general secretary of the World Council of Churches, announced the creation of an Eminent Persons Ecumenical Program for Africa. According to a media report, "The persons will be available at short-notice for deployment to trouble spots, where they will use their training, experience and status to engage in peace talks as well as make recommendations for action by governmental bodies and ecumenical agencies." At the parish level, St. Bartholomew's Episcopal Church in New York has created its own initiative for bridging interfaith differences. Its Center for Religious Inquiry is led by a rabbi, taught by academics and intended to promote deeper understanding among different faiths.

There have been encouraging efforts even within Sudan. Unlike Khartoum, where Christian leaders showed me little interest in reconciliation, the south of the country has known significant interfaith cooperation. The New Sudan Council of Churches has worked on issues of reconciliation, and Paride Taban resigned as bishop of the Catholic Diocese of Torit to create a Peace Village to deal with the legacy of ethnic and religious conflict and to promote the healing of the country. The International Center for Religion and Diplomacy, led by Douglas Johnston, is doing impressive work in focusing on religion as a cause of conflict and potential source of reconciliation in various parts of the world, including Sudan.

More generally, we should be open to a variety of ideas on how religion might help resolve political conflict. For example, there might be an effective way for leaders of different faiths to join in condemning terrorism, and for insisting that civilian immunity from attack is a widely held religious principle. The starting point is the recognition that throughout history, religion has been a cause of bloodshed, and it remains so today. Because religion has contributed to the world's problems, it must develop specific and practical ways to help solve those problems.

For decades, Sudan has been a tragedy of conflict and bloodshed, where religion has been a component, if not the cause, of the conflict. The Reverend Michael Perry, the very impressive Franciscan priest and Africa Desk Coordinator for Franciscans International, is dedicated to the ministry of reconciliation and sees Sudan as more than a tragedy. In his words, "Sudan is an opportunity for religious groups to demonstrate what they can do. Sudan is a moment of history for religious groups. Is there sufficient will within the religious community to collaborate as never before?" If there is, he continues, "Sudan could be a model for religion in the rest of the world." I agree with Father Perry. Sudan is a tragedy in its own right, but it is also a challenge to people of faith to demonstrate the will to become peacemakers.

Michael Perry believes that a sustained religious commitment to the ministry of reconciliation is essential, and that such an effort should be supported by governments and by international institutions. I agree with that as well, which is why I pressed the notion of a mediation entity while serving the United States at the United Nations. But without waiting for governments to help, religious people should make a more intense effort to be peacemakers, beginning in Sudan. Michael Perry is quite correct. Sudan is a moment of history.

AMERICAN COMPASSION TOWARD A SUFFERING WORLD

"For if you love those who love you, what reward do you have? Do not even the tax collectors do the same? And if you greet only your brothers and sisters, what more are you doing than others? Do not even the Gentiles do the same?"

—MATTHEW 5:46–47

CAMBODIA, 1979

When religion is at its best, compassion is its gift to American politics. It is compassion offered for its own sake and not with the hope of getting something in return, so it transcends concerns about national self-interest. As the story of the Good Samaritan and the above-quoted verses from the Sermon on the Mount tell us, this compassion is not confined to loving people who love us in return or who bear any resemblance to us. It is religion's gift to politics, but it is not politics. It is the weight people of faith put on the scales of government, but the scales of government bear other weights as well. And though compassion is a gift religion brings to politics, it is not an unalloyed offering. It is easily adulterated and transformed by other attributes religious people sometimes bring to politics: self-righteousness, judgmentalism and an ambition to claim their own special places in God's kingdom.

I saw religion at its best in 1979 when people of faith responded to massive starvation in Cambodia. That country had endured unbelievable suffering since its brutal dictator, Pol Pot, came to power in 1975, and established his Khmer Rouge regime. He created the notorious killing fields of Cambodia, massacring people he perceived as opponents, including intellectuals, whom he defined as people who wore eyeglasses. As an agrarian movement, the Khmer Rouge evacuated the capital city of Phnom Penh, forcing its residents to leave their homes and go into the countryside with no means to support themselves. Then in December 1978, the government of Vietnam, hardly a regime friendly to the United States, invaded Cambodia in order to oust the Khmer Rouge. The fighting that ensued disrupted farming, leading to a massive shortfall in food production. The routed Khmer Rouge and many others made the long trek across much of their country to reach the safety of the border of Thailand, many of them dying of starvation or disease along the way.

At the time, I was a freshman senator who knew next to nothing about Cambodia. The turning point for me was an opinion piece in the long since defunct *Washington Star* written by the liberal Catholic columnist Mary McGrory, who made a direct appeal to people of faith to save the dying people of Cambodia. In an article entitled "Is It Christian to Let People Starve?" her point was not subtle. How, she asked, could Christians do nothing when so many people were dying? I took the point personally. It was a question from a Christian to a Christian. Where was I, and how could I stand by when countless people were dying?

The day after I read Mary McGrory's column, I spoke to Senator Howard Baker, then the Republican leader of the Senate. I told him that I had been moved by what I had read in the paper, and I urged him to go to Cambodia. He immediately turned the tables on me. In a response characteristic of the finest person I knew in the Senate, he said, "You should go there. I'll see if Bob Byrd (Senate Majority Leader Robert Byrd, D-WV) will authorize an air force plane." Then, as the excellent photographer he is, he added, "You should take a camera and take a lot of pictures of what you see."

Three nights later, I was on a plane, leaving Andrews Air Force Base with fellow senators Jim Sasser of Tennessee and Max Baucus of Montana. Both were Democrats, but partisanship was not a factor. We headed for Bangkok, Thailand, our jumping-off point for trips to the border of Thailand and Cambodia and on into Phnom Penh. With us was then assistant secretary of state Richard Holbrooke, later one of my predecessors as ambassador to the United Nations and my much-admired friend. A brief exchange with Holbrooke during that long plane ride has stayed with me ever since. I said, "I don't know what to do when we get there." He replied, "When you see it, you will know what to do."

We saw it. The highly capable U.S. ambassador to Thailand, Morton Abramowitz, took us to the Cambodian border, where we saw people by the thousands—mostly women, children and the elderly. We saw people lying in the grass too weak to get food just steps away. We saw people dying on the ground in pools of their own urine, and babies dying in their mothers' arms. We saw children with the distended bellies and reddish hair of malnutrition with flies on their faces, listless, staring blankly. There was silence—no animation, no talking. And we saw the advance contingent of volunteers, many westerners, representatives of the International

Committee of the Red Cross (ICRC), Oxfam International and other organizations struggling to save as many lives as they could.

Richard Holbrooke was correct. When we saw it, we knew what to do. Along with a foreign service officer and a military attaché, who, as an accommodation to the media, carried a television camera, Senators Sasser, Baucus and I flew to Phnom Penh, the first governmental delegation of Americans to go there since the Khmer Rouge had seized power four years earlier. By all appearances, the city had once been beautiful, with broad, tree-lined boulevards reminiscent of its French colonial past. Now this city that had once housed hundreds of thousands was deserted. No people. No traffic. I stood in the middle of a boulevard and took pictures in both directions. Nothing. In Phnom Penh, we met with Hun Sen, a former low-level officer in the Khmer Rouge who, after defecting to Vietnam, had been appointed foreign minister of the Vietnamese-installed People's Republic of Kampuchea. We urged him to allow a land bridge, caravans of trucks carrying food to enter Cambodia from Thailand, an idea first articulated by Ambassador Abramowitz. Failing to get that permission, we did what we could to get as much food as possible to the border, where it could be carried into Cambodia.

Before leaving Bangkok, I had a clear vision of what had to be done on our return to Washington. I recall telling an aide, "Apart from marrying Sally, this is the most important thing I have ever done."

Following Howard Baker's advice, I took many rolls of pictures, which I hurriedly had developed the day we returned to Washington. That same day, Jim Sasser, Max Baucus and I met President Carter in the Cabinet Room of the White House, presented a slide show of our trip, and appealed for more food aid for

Cambodia. The following day, we three senators testified before the Senate Foreign Relations Committee, and again presented slides of what we had seen. Dan Rather showed the pictures on the *CBS Evening News.* During these same days, film shot by camera crews that had accompanied us to the Thai-Cambodian border was appearing on television. As a result, what had been an obscure story of suffering in Cambodia became national news. The response of the American people who sent contributions to the Red Cross and other nongovernmental organizations was heartwarming. Schoolchildren from outside of Kansas City wrote to tell me of a car wash they had held to raise funds. Fourth graders at the St. Joseph Institute for the Deaf in St. Louis County, kids with their own problems, sent me a check for twenty-three dollars and some odd cents together with a note. They told me it was Thanksgiving time, and they were counting their own blessings. They were concerned about the children of Cambodia, so they had taken a collection to help them. They asked me to put the money in the right hands. Four days after our return to Washington, President Carter instructed Richard Holbrooke to return to the region, this time with the president's wife, Rosalynn. With White House support, Congress passed a $30 million emergency supplemental appropriation for humanitarian assistance to the Cambodians.

Twenty-seven years after my Cambodian experience, three thoughts come to mind that, for me, have meaning beyond that time and place. First, the experience was expressly religious. People of faith saw the religious dimension and took action. Mary McGrory's column was not for everybody. It was an intentionally religious call to action. More specific, it was written by a Christian to Christians. The collection taken by the fourth graders at the St. Joseph Institute for the Deaf was more than sentimental. As they said in their note to me, it was a thanksgiving for their own blessings from children attending a religious school. Many people who contacted me did so as a witness to their faith. Churches asked me to speak. Charles Perry, then provost of the Washington National Cathedral, arranged a service especially for Cambodia and another service on the general subject of world hunger.

I do not mean to imply that only religious people respond to the kind of human disaster I saw in Cambodia. Certainly, that is not the case. I am sure that the volunteers I saw on the border of Thailand represented a variety of religions as well as no religion at all. Plenty of kind, decent, caring people have no religious beliefs, and they act out of the goodness of their hearts. Conversely, plenty of people who profess to be religious, even those who worship regularly, show no particular interest in the world beyond themselves. But caring for people in need is a central requirement of every religion I know about, and as Mary McGrory clearly saw, it is certainly a central requirement for Christians. Many people who responded to Cambodia were acting out their faith, and our government's efforts to help the Cambodians reflected the values of those people.

My second thought about our response to Cambodia is how closely it followed the above-quoted verses from the Sermon on the Mount, "If you greet only your brothers and sisters, what more are you doing than others?" It is difficult to imagine any people more different from average Americans than the Cambodians of 1979. Their country was halfway around the world. Probably few Americans had ever seen a Cambodian. Many of the people who were dying at the border of Thailand had followed the unimaginably brutal dictator Pol Pot. They were Khmer Rouge. The people who chased them out of their country were the Vietnamese

Communists that Americans had been fighting a few years earlier. America had no remaining political or strategic interest in what was happening in Cambodia. We responded solely because the dying people of Cambodia, whatever their distance from us, whatever their politics, were children of God, and we saw it as our duty to try to save them.

The third point that sticks in my mind is the advice Richard Holbrooke gave me as we flew to Bangkok: "When you see it, you will know what to do." In other words, it was all right not to have a prearranged plan to be implemented when we reached our destination. We could trust our instincts. What we took to Thailand and Cambodia was concern, not an agenda. We wanted to do what we could to help the people of Cambodia, but we had no idea of what might be effective. When we saw the suffering, we responded to what we saw and developed a plan, the proposed land bridge of trucks carrying food into Cambodia. It seemed to us a workable idea, and we did our best to persuade Vietnamese authorities to implement it. We did not succeed in sending in convoys of trucks.

But the specifics of the plan for a land bridge were secondary to our concern for the people we saw on the border of Thailand. The plan was only a means to an end. When we failed to get permission to send in truckloads of food, we tried a different approach. We focused world attention on Cambodia; we showed our pictures to the president, to a Senate committee and—thanks to network news—to the American people. We visited the United Nations. We used every means we could think of to increase the amount of food aid going to the people of Cambodia and to put pressure on the government of Vietnam to let food reach the people. The result was more food at the border and a kind of land bridge, although less than what we had sought. Food was carried into Cambodia, but it was in carts and on people's backs rather than in trucks. I have no doubt that the attention we focused on Cambodia helped save countless lives.

The lesson I learned is the difference between agenda and concern. It was a critical difference when we responded to the crisis in Cambodia. Had we been intent on a fixed agenda, on a land bridge of trucks, we would have failed, however desirable that agenda was. Concern for dying people preceded the formulation of a specific plan, caused the plan to come into being, and survived the failure of the plan. Concern rather than an agenda appealed to the conscience of the world, increased food aid, caused deaf children in St. Louis to send in their allowance money and saved the lives of dying people.

The difference between agenda and concern is critical as we think about religion's gift to politics. We often speak about the religious agenda or the Christian agenda in politics, as though there were a detailed, God-approved plan of action that it is our duty to implement. If there is such a plan, then someone should be able to tell us what it is, just as Richard Holbrooke might have told us how to save the Cambodians before our plane touched down at the Bangkok airport. If there is such a plan, we might find it in the Bible, or be instructed in it by a church hierarchy, or be expected to follow it by television personalities. If there is such a plan, there might be a religious way to vote, or more narrowly, a Christian way to vote, with Christian candidates and Christian political platforms.

That is one view of religion and politics. But while Richard Holbrooke was not speaking about religion, I think his advice was closer to the mark. "When you see it, you will know what to do."

When you see your neighbors, their needs, their joys, their sorrows, when you see them next door or halfway around the world, you will know what to do. It is concern that precedes and inspires agendas, and survives when agendas fail, and it causes us to try again, always trying our best, never certain about our own judgment. It is knowing that God's purpose exceeds whatever we can put in an agenda. For Christians, it is trusting in the guidance of the Holy Spirit.

SUDAN, 2001–2005

In a White House Rose Garden ceremony on September 6, 2001, five days before terrorists attacked America, President George W. Bush named me his special envoy for peace in Sudan. Cynics have suggested that America's engagement in Sudan was driven by our need for that country's oil production. But whatever oil Sudan could produce is such a miniscule percent of our consumption that I give no weight to the suspicions of the cynics. Certainly, our country had an interest in gaining Sudan's cooperation in our efforts against terrorism. Moreover, President Bush saw the prospect of peace in Sudan as a possible model for resolving ethnic and religious conflicts in the Middle East and elsewhere. As the president once said to me, "If they [the Sudanese] can figure it out, anyone can."

But the energy fueling our effort in Sudan was clear to me when I saw the Christian leaders in the audience that day and when I considered the religious convictions of President Bush. American Christians wanted our government to make every effort to end the world's longest lasting civil war, which was said to have claimed some two million lives. Much of the impetus behind America's renewed effort to bring peace to Sudan came from evangelical Protestants who had heard that Sudan's Islamic government was persecuting black Africans, many of whom were Christian. But concern for the Sudanese was a common thread that ran through the various branches of Christianity. During my service as special envoy, I met with Christians ranging from the Reverend Franklin Graham, who operates a medical ministry in southern Sudan, to clergy and laypeople in my own Episcopal Church who traveled to that country, to a committee of Catholic bishops. There are significant differences among various kinds of Christians in their religious beliefs and in their understandings of the appropriate relationship between religion and politics. Concern for the suffering of Sudan is an example of the shared compassion that holds people of faith together.

Like Cambodia, Sudan is dramatically different from the United States, again evoking in Christians the words from the Sermon on the Mount, "If you love those who love you, what reward do you have?" Most Sudanese don't love the United States or even know about the United States. Khartoum, the capital, once home to Osama bin Laden, is a third world, predominantly Muslim city situated where the White Nile and Blue Nile converge to create the grotesquely polluted Nile River. Its few paved streets are clogged with various kinds of vehicles: cars, trucks and donkey carts. Its government, long subject to a broad range of economic sanctions imposed by the United States, remains on our list of countries that have provided aid to terrorists, although, since 9/11, many American officials believe that the government of Sudan has been reasonably cooperative in our antiterrorism efforts. Two days before

I flew into Karida, in the hotly contested Nuba Mountains area of central Sudan, government troops fired three artillery rounds in the direction of a World Food Program plane that had made an advance trip to the landing area. Those were obviously warning shots across my bow. To say the least, the relationship between the United States and the government of Sudan has not been friendly. However, I proceeded with my visit to the Nuba Mountains, which went off peacefully. For the first time, the government of Sudan authorized food flights to the beleaguered population. It was an important first step for my mission.

Outside Khartoum, the country is almost wholly undeveloped. In the south of Sudan, an immense geographical area that fought a twenty-one year civil war of secession, there are no paved roads. People live in small communities of huts made out of sticks. In virtually all of the south, there is no electricity and no means of communication. On a visit to Rumbek, in the rebel-held south, a guide walked me down the dirt road that ran through the town, and pointed to a man sitting in the dust making flip-flops out of the tread of an abandoned tire. "That's the shoe factory," he said. It was difficult for me to understand how the rebels could succeed in transforming the landlocked south of Sudan into a viable country, even if they were to win the war.

One experience especially exemplifies the vast cultural distance that separates the Sudanese from Americans who care so much about them. I had flown into a rebel-held part of the Nuba Mountains, and landed in an open field where the rebel army had gathered thousands of people from the countryside to greet me. Sweeping long sticks in front of them, the soldiers herded the crowd to the front of a tarpaulin-covered stage that had been erected for the occasion. Some of the crowd climbed trees to see what was happening. First, a politician from the SPLM made a well-received speech, which, while I could not understand the language, impressed me with its high volume and intensity. Then I was asked to speak. I told them my name, and said I had come from the United States because President Bush had sent me. As I was speaking, Jon Sawyer, a reporter from the *St. Louis Post-Dispatch*, circulated in the audience with an interpreter asking people at random three questions: "Do you know who that is?" "Do you know who President Bush is?" "Do you know what the United States is?" In every interview, the answer was the same to each question: no. No one had the slightest idea who President Bush was, or what the United States is, or why I was there. I am sure they had no idea why they were there, except that the soldiers had made them come.

The role of a special envoy is to be the personal representative of the president of the United States. I worked closely with Ambassador Michael Ranneberger; deputy assistant secretary of state, Charles Snyder; deputy administrator of the United States Agency for International Development, Roger Winter; and Jeff Millington, America's coordinator for Sudan Affairs, during the negotiations. Early in my efforts, I received invaluable advice from my good friend and former ambassador to Zaire, Somalia and Pakistan, Robert Oakley. But as I frequently told Sudanese on both sides of the civil war, I was not part of the State Department, and my presence demonstrated the personal engagement of President Bush in helping bring peace to their country. That personal engagement was very real. Every time I went to Sudan or to neighboring Kenya, where the peace talks were being held, I spoke in advance with the president, either in person in the Oval Office or by telephone, and received from him the message I should convey to the parties. At one point during my service, I wrote a progress report of about thirty pages, which I assumed White House staff would digest into a page or two and transmit to the president. When I met with him to discuss my recommendations, the president said, "Good report. Very well written." He had not relied on a staff-prepared summary. He had read the report.

My understanding of the mission President Bush gave me differed from the expectations of concerned American Christians, especially members of Congress who had long been committed to a deeper American involvement in Sudan. Soon after the president named me his special envoy, I visited individually with members of Congress who had made Sudan their issue. Many of the visits were remarkably similar, with congressmen using the same phrase in their efforts to educate me about the conflict. They said, "There is no moral equivalence between the SPLM and the government of Sudan." In other words, the government was the oppressor, and the southern Sudanese were the victims.

I did not doubt this observation, but I did not think it relevant to my mission. As I understood it, President Bush had asked me to see if America could be a peacemaker. He did not ask me to be the moral arbiter between the two sides. The Clinton administration had gotten nowhere with the parties by weighing in very heavily on the side of the SPLM and against the government. That approach does have the advantage of taking a clear moral position, and it has great appeal to religious people who want America to be the champion of the oppressed and to speak out against the oppressor. But my job, as I saw it, was not to make moral judgments, however warranted they would have been. My job was to help move the parties toward a just peace. In my view, it would not have helped the goal of successful negotiations for the United States to announce that it was firmly in favor of one side. Any successful ne-

gotiation entails give-and-take on every side. In the difficult negotiations ahead, involving complex issues of power sharing, wealth
sharing, and the rights of southerners to determine their future,
the effective strategy was not to say that one side was morally right
and the other side was morally wrong.

I made my goal of practical results, as opposed to moral procla-
mations, clear on my first visit to the SPLM stronghold of Rumbek. My fellow Episcopalians had invited me to speak at a late
afternoon service at their cathedral. It turned out that this was an
open-air service in the shade of a huge spreading tree with several
hundred people sitting on wood plank benches. The former cathedral had been destroyed by bombing. I had a clear idea of what I
wanted to say in the homily I was to give, and when I asked for a
Bible, Roger Winter produced a small New Testament from his
briefcase. I spoke about the fourth chapter of John's Gospel, the
account of Jesus and the woman at the well. The story is that Jesus,
tired and thirsty, arrived at noontime at Jacob's well. When a Samaritan woman came to fill her water jar, Jesus made a simple request, "Give me a drink." Instead of offering him the water, the
woman engaged Jesus in debate. The sayings that follow—Jesus is
the source of "living water," "God is spirit, and those who worship
him must worship in spirit and truth"—are the point of the story.
But the focus of my homily was on the behavior of the woman.
Jesus had a need. He was thirsty, and he asked for a drink. The
woman did not give him a drink. She gave him talk. After decades
of fighting and years of talking about peace, it was time to end the
talking and get on with the peace. It was a message to both the
government of Sudan and the SPLM.

The summer after my appointment as special envoy, the government of Sudan's top representative in the United States, Ahmed

Khidir, flew to St. Louis to have lunch with me. He told me that his foreign minister had instructed him to ask me one question, which was, "Is it the position of the United States government that we're damned if we do and damned if we don't?" In other words, he wanted to know whether the United States was so locked into its opposition to the government of Sudan that it would do no good in its relations with the United States to make concessions that might lead to peace. I told Mr. Khidir that I would relay the foreign minister's question directly to President Bush. I did that in a meeting in the Oval Office immediately before my next trip to Khartoum, and in Khartoum I delivered President Bush's response to the president of Sudan, Omar al-Bashir.

President Bush's answer was that he wanted to achieve normal relations with Sudan, assuming (1) a peace agreement between the government and the SPLM, (2) complete access for humanitarian workers throughout the country and (3) total cooperation in the war against terrorism. I am convinced that the response of President Bush was a critical factor in persuading the government of Sudan to make the concessions that led to the peace agreement signed by the parties in January 2005.

The United States did not take part in the peace process as a moral arbiter, nor did we do so as a know-it-all. We did not offer our own peace plan. We worked closely with neighboring African countries and their designated mediator, my candidate for the Nobel Peace Prize, General Lazaro Sumbeiywo of Kenya. We worked with other engaged countries, especially Norway and the United Kingdom. We did everything we could to convey the message that the world cared about Sudan, and that the world would respond favorably to peace.

Every month, the presidency of the United Nations Security

Council rotates in alphabetical sequence to one of its members. November 2004 was our turn, and at that time I had the honor of representing the United States in the United Nations. Since the UN's founding in 1945, the Security Council had met outside of New York City on only three other occasions, and there was resistance to doing so again, both among council members and in Washington. But this was the time to make a statement that the world was watching the negotiations, and the world wanted peace. So the Security Council of the United Nations went to Nairobi, Kenya, and there adopted a resolution we had negotiated on the U.S. Air Force plane that had taken us to our destination. Our membership had diverse interests. Algeria represented Arab countries. Angola and Benin represented black Africa. China had oil interests in Sudan, and was generally disposed to favor the Sudanese government. We unanimously adopted our resolution. Its importance was not in its specifics, which we had wordsmithed on the plane. Its importance was that we spoke with one voice. And, as one, we stood behind a table as the leader of the SPLM and the vice president of Sudan signed a promise they kept two months later: to reach a peace agreement.

Had the United States seen its role as making moral statements, we would have given no reason for the government of Sudan to engage in negotiations leading to a peace agreement. Had we seen our task in the Security Council as championing one side against the other, we would have forced a no vote from Algeria and a probable veto from China. Domestically in the United States, that strategy would have had great appeal, especially to people of various faiths who were moved by the suffering in Sudan and wanted to speak out against injustice, but it would have set back the peace process.

"Peace process" is the applicable term, for peace is an ongoing work, not a final achievement. The agreement between the government of Sudan and the SPLM was signed in a sports stadium in Nairobi under a brilliant blue sky on January 9, 2005. Heads of state from many African countries witnessed the signing, as did high officials from the United Kingdom and Norway. Secretary of State Colin Powell represented the United States, as did members of the American team who had devoted their talents and energy to making the day possible. Sitting on the platform behind Colin Powell, taking in the jubilation of Sudanese as they danced on the stadium infield, I thought that it was one of the most eventful days of my life. I had been working for this day for more than three years. I had made nine or ten hard trips to Africa as well as some trips to Europe. I had shuttled back and forth between the two sides, encouraging them to give a little more, to consider new ideas, to reach compromises. And now, at last, peace had come, and in that festive stadium a new Sudan was born.

It was a great day, but fleeting euphoria gave way to stark reality. As the ceremony in Nairobi was ending the world's longest civil war, a new civil war was raging in the Darfur region of western Sudan, so even with the end of one war, there was no peace in that country. To suppress an uprising of black Africans in Darfur, the government had armed nomadic Arabs known as Jinjaweed, who proceeded to attack, rape and pillage the blacks. This new civil war threatened to be even more difficult to resolve than the war that had just ended. Instead of two parties that could negotiate with each other, the rebels in Darfur were divided into factions that argued among themselves, and the government of Sudan claimed it could not control the Jinjaweed it had armed.

So now the attention of the United States and the rest of the world has turned to Darfur. The United Nations Security Council has passed several resolutions calling on the parties to reach a peace agreement and threatening unspecified "measures" against the government of Sudan. Many people have suggested that such measures include economic sanctions against Sudan, but since the government now includes the SPLM, and since China would surely exercise the veto, economic sanctions are not a realistic option. With logistical support from the United States, the African Union has deployed some seven thousand troops to Darfur, which should soon be incorporated into a UN peacekeeping force. From time to time, American editorial writers and columnists opine that the United States should not stand idly by while the people of Darfur suffer, but they do not spell out what they think our government should do. It is certain that we are not standing idly by. Secretaries of state Colin Powell and Condoleezza Rice have traveled to Darfur, and the deputy secretary of state, Robert Zoellick, has gone there repeatedly to try to encourage peace. Some columnists have seemed to suggest that the United States should send troops to Darfur, but since the beginning of the Iraq War, there has been no chance that the United States unilaterally would invade and maintain a long-term occupation of a predominantly Muslim country, even to help the suffering people of Darfur.

As Darfur presents its own tragedies, peace in the rest of the country is a work in progress. Six months after the agreement in Nairobi was signed, a new government was established in Khartoum, which included John Garang, the great leader of the SPLM, as first vice president. But three weeks later, Garang was killed while flying in bad weather in a Ugandan helicopter. Still, the agreement is holding. Recognizing the importance of demonstrating the fruits of peace, interested countries including the United States met in Oslo, Norway, in April 2005 and committed $4.5 billion toward the development of Sudan. The United States pledged $1.7 billion of that amount, but in making the pledge, Deputy Secretary Zoellick made an obvious point. The future of Sudan as a whole and the situation in Darfur are closely linked to each other. The United States cannot commit funds through the government of Sudan so long as that government is a party to the horrors of Darfur.

Sudan is a large, very poor and very complex country in which peace is never accomplished easily, and certainly not by the signing of an agreement. If Sudan is to have a future of hope, it will require the long-term attention of the rest of the world, especially the United States. The Security Council will not impose economic sanctions against Sudan, but it will continue to keep the problems of Sudan on the world stage, just as it did when it met in Nairobi in 2004.

As far as the United States is concerned, engagement with Sudan, although essential to that nation's future, cannot be justified solely by the requirements of our national self-interest. Sudan has little impact on the security or economic concerns of America. That means that our engagement with Sudan will depend on our values, on our compassion for human suffering, and that kind of compassion is the gift of religion to American politics.

COMBATING CHARACTER ASSASSINATION

Historians tell us there is nothing new about the politics of smear. Countless incidents support their claims. They point, for example, to the 1884 presidential campaign when the bachelor candidate, Grover Cleveland, faced charges that he had fathered a child out of wedlock. The tradition continues. In 2004, Democrats attacked George W. Bush's service in the National Guard while swift boat veterans challenged John Kerry's record in Vietnam. However effective these various attacks might have been in changing votes, they hardly related to the great issues that faced the country.

Politics has been so dirty for so long that most candidates for elective office expect that attacks will follow filing for public office. Still, even for professional politicians, the severity of the attack can come as a shock. My friend Tom Eagleton had survived campaigns for circuit attorney, attorney general, lieutenant governor and U.S. senator before the horrible ordeal of being forced from the McGovern ticket in 1972 by stories that he had received psychiatric treatment. Senator John Tower of Texas was one of the toughest politicians I knew. A self-assured Texan who could do battle with anyone, he was the first President Bush's nominee for secretary of defense whose confirmation was defeated after a public campaign accusing him of womanizing and excessive drinking. His ordeal extended over a period of weeks with daily newspaper and television stories of his alleged misdeeds. When his misery finally ended in defeat, he arrived one Tuesday at the weekly Republican policy lunch, an occasion he had presided over during his years in the Senate. After the meal, he sought recognition, then stood to thank his former colleagues for the support they had given him. But words failed him. The self-assured, tough-talking Texan broke down in tears.

Bush, Kerry, Eagleton and Tower had spent many years becoming callused to the rough world of politics. Men and women recruited from private life by presidents to serve in appointed positions lack the calluses of professional politicians and can be caught unaware by the ferocity of the attacks. In 1999, some Republican senators opposed President Clinton's nomination of a sixty-six-year-old, openly gay philanthropist, James Hormel, as ambassador to Luxembourg. In the campaign to defeat the Hormel nomination, the executive director of the Traditional Values Coalition accused him of being a "purveyor of smut" and of "cheering on child molesters and transvestite nuns." According to one press report, the efforts of the Traditional Values Coalition included distributing to members of the Senate a sexually explicit coloring book.

One Republican senator compared Hormel to David Duke, former grand wizard of the Ku Klux Klan. All this in an effort to block a nomination for ambassador to the tiny country of Luxembourg.

Another example of attempting to defeat a nominee by destroying his reputation involved a man who had been nominated to what I would call a second-tier position in a Republican administration. I do not recall the nominee's name or whether this occurred during the Reagan or George H. W. Bush administration. What is relevant is how he was attacked when his name reached the Senate floor.

All people who are nominated by presidents for government positions undergo background checks by the FBI, during which they answer extensive questions about their lives. One of the standard questions goes to past drug use. When the background check is complete, its findings are shared with the Senate in a highly confidential manner. An FBI agent, accompanied by a representative of the White House, delivers the report in a plain envelope to the office of one senator from each of the two parties, usually the chairman and ranking minority member of the committee with jurisdiction over the nomination. Each senator reading the report must do so in the presence of the FBI and White House personnel and is prohibited from copying the report.

In cases of nominees who were of college age in the 1960s and later, acknowledgment of some past drug use is common to the point of being expected, assuming absolute candor in providing information to the FBI. I certainly did not view it as a disqualification for a federal job, provided the drug use was experimental and not continuing. But while not a disqualification, it was the sort of embarrassment most people would not like to have publicly known, especially by their children.

The individual whose confirmation was before the Senate was middle-aged and had two children. He had admitted in his confidential forms to twice experimenting with cocaine as a young man. That admission, which was incorporated into the FBI report, was carried by the media. The only reasonable explanation for the media's receiving the cocaine story is that a senator who had seen the FBI report had leaked it, in violation of federal criminal law and Senate rules. The senator could have been censured by or even expelled from the Senate and prosecuted by the Justice Department, but neither punishment occurred. The reason was that the media that received the leak protected its source. I went to the Senate chamber and made a speech denouncing the leak while the senator I believed was responsible was on the floor, but that was of little comfort to the nominee whose reputation had been sullied. The senator who leaked the information did so with impunity.

Two points about the character assassination of presidential nominees deserve mention. First, in submitting themselves to the confirmation process, most nominees have a great deal to lose. Almost by definition, those appointed by the president of the United States to offices high enough to require Senate confirmation are people of accomplishment who have spent lifetimes building reputations of which they are proud. When they fall, it is from positions of height, often very great height. Second, their downfall is very visible. It is a matter not of private misfortune but of public disgrace. It is carried in the media, sometimes on national television. The media would claim that these stories of ruined reputations are newsworthy. Perhaps. Certainly such stories make good copy. Sometimes they help defeat nominees of whom editorialists disapprove.

To supplement whatever the "free" media reports, groups seeking to defeat a nominee can avail themselves of the "paid" media by purchasing newspaper ads or running television commercials attacking a nominee's reputation. The use of television commercials to attack reputations has become a common tactic in efforts to defeat nominees for the U.S. Supreme Court, where, since the nomination of Robert Bork, the confirmation process has resembled political campaigns.

The most famous attempt to destroy a Supreme Court nominee is one with which I was intimately familiar: the 1991 confirmation of Clarence Thomas. I wrote a book entitled *Resurrection*, which set out the details of that dramatic episode as I saw them, so I will not rehash them here, except to say that two days before the scheduled Senate vote, with confirmation all but assured, National Public Radio broke a story that Thomas had allegedly made sexually suggestive comments to a person he had supervised at the Department of Education. For several reasons set out in *Resurrection*, I am convinced that Clarence Thomas did not act improperly. But the charges and countercharges of the time are not relevant here. What is relevant is the effect of this sad ordeal on a person I know and care about.

My friend Clarence felt publicly disgraced. As he told me at the time, he felt that the charge had put a stain on him that he could never remove. For sheer agony, I wonder if anything matches the experience of personal disgrace, especially when one has spent a lifetime building a reputation and when the fall is covered by network news. For more than a week, Clarence could not sleep. He barely ate. He could not keep still, alternately standing and sitting, his hands always in motion. He was frequently in tears, not quietly crying but loudly sobbing. What made the experience so heartbreaking was that it involved one of the most kind and gentle people I know.

I have known Clarence Thomas since he was a third-year student at Yale Law School whom I recruited to work in my office when I was attorney general of Missouri. I hired him again to be a legislative assistant when I was in the Senate. Any number of stories could illustrate my impression of Clarence the person and why I and so many people who know him well feel strongly about him and rallied to his defense when he was before the Senate in 1991. I will relate but one such story.

A few years ago, my wife, Sally, and I attended a speech Clarence made in a school gymnasium in St. Louis. Perhaps three hundred people were in attendance. After the speech and question and answer period, many of the departing crowd gathered around Clarence to speak to him privately, as Sally and I stood a short distance away, waiting to drive him to our home. His eyes focused intently as each person in turn engaged him in sometimes extended conversation. Two adults and a boy, perhaps eleven or twelve years old, approached Clarence. The adults were white. The child appeared to be African American. For maybe ten minutes, Clarence and the boy spoke directly to each other, as though no one else were in the gym. Finally, the family turned away, the boy walking past Sally and me with tears running down his face. On the way to our home, we asked Clarence about the boy and were told that he was of mixed race and attended a predominantly white school. He had shared with Clarence his thoughts about his own identity and his emotional struggle as a mixed-race child in a white environment.

We stayed in that school gym until every person who wanted to speak to Clarence had done so. We were the last people to leave that night. By the time we departed, the custodians had stacked the folding chairs on which the audience had sat.

———

It is easy to become so involved with our political causes that we assume anything goes if it advances those causes. When attacks shift from issues to personalities, we forget that real people become the targets, real people who are children of God. Real people suffer pain.

After the Senate's vote on Clarence Thomas, I focused my attention on the procedural shortcomings of confirmation proceedings. Nominees are on trial, not for their lives but for their reputations, for what makes their lives worth living. But unlike court trials, hearings before Senate committees have none of the attributes of due process. Nominees are not represented by counsel, and they do not cross-examine their accusers. They have no power to interview witnesses in advance of the hearings or to compel the production of records. So I reasoned that the Senate should adopt new procedures for confirmation hearings when serious charges were made against nominees. The new procedures would formalize the hearings, so they are more like trials. Most important, I thought that nominees should be able to retain counsel at government expense and that counsel should be able to cross-examine witnesses. Sometime after Clarence's confirmation, I offered an amendment to that effect on the Senate floor. My proposed amendment was defeated by a wide margin, I suppose because my colleagues thought that offering it was sour grapes on my part. Whatever the reason and regardless of my belief that confirmation hearings should take place with more due process protections, I am resigned to the conclusion that the Senate will remain as it is and will resist transforming its hearings into a more trial-like system.

My resignation about the possibilities of procedural changes to protect nominees does not mean that I have given up on making

———

confirmation hearings less vicious and more fair. In fact, I think that real reform can be achieved not so much by changing the rules as by changing the hearts of the American people. Those who practice character assassination must believe that it works. They must think that the public accepts it, that perhaps the public is titillated by it, that the public will become so indignant at the nominee as to demand that senators vote against confirmation.

My hope is that having seen character assassination repeatedly in the confirmation process, having been surfeited by it, the American people will begin responding in a way that is just the opposite of what its practitioners expect. My hope is that their response will be revulsion—revulsion to the point of nausea. When the American people so respond, the system will change.

To date, most examples of attacks on the character of judicial nominees have been cases of liberal groups' trying to defeat conservatives. Their reasoning might be, "We really can't stand more conservative justices on the Supreme Court. This is very bad for the country, and we have a responsibility to try to stop it. So, if it takes a personal attack on an individual to save the country from a conservative court, so be it." In other words, the rationale might be that the end justifies the means.

But the tactic of destroying reputations to accomplish philosophical objectives is not the sole possession of Democrats or liberals. Sooner or later, there will be a Democratic president who will nominate liberal justices. When that day comes, I have no doubt that conservatives will remember the confirmation battles over Bork and Thomas and think that it is payback time.

If the confirmation process is wrong when liberals are attacking conservatives, it will be wrong when conservatives are attacking liberals. If it is right now, it will be right then. So it is important that the American people look at the current state of Supreme Court confirmations, not from the standpoint of their own political philosophies, but in light of their tolerance for or revulsion at character assassination. My hope is that in the near future, Americans will decide that the interest groups that control the confirmation process have gone too far and that the current system must change.

But if the confirmation of presidential nominees, especially Supreme Court nominees, is no more than a struggle for partisan or ideological advantage, the system will not change. Today, liberal opponents of the president's choices have a stake in the status quo. In a few years, it may be the conservatives who want to destroy the reputations of liberals. If an outcry is going to arise against the miserable state of the confirmation process, it will come from the public, not from the political professionals.

Some church groups were interested in the confirmation of Clarence Thomas as advocates for one side or the other. But I do not recall any outrage expressed by people of faith against the confirmation process itself. This is a subject that is ripe for religious leadership. It might even be an area in which liberal, moderate and conservative Christians could find agreement and work together for change.

The prophetic tradition of the Bible speaks in both broad and narrow terms. It broadly condemns oppression of the poor and needy, and it expresses outrage at the abuse of specific individuals. In 2 Samuel 11, when Nathan confronted King David, he did not voice a general complaint about a social policy. David had committed a particular wrong against a particular person. Having committed adultery with Bathsheba, David ordered her husband, Uriah, sent into battle to be killed so that David could claim Uriah's wife.

In 1 Kings 21, when Elijah condemned King Ahab, it had nothing to do with political policy. Ahab's wife, Jezebel, had their neighbor Naboth stoned to death in order to seize his vineyard.

Speaking out on issues of public policy is clearly within the prophetic tradition, but it does not exhaust the prophetic tradition. We do not discharge responsibility to our neighbor if we support some legislative initiative that affects the population at large, but are silent about the suffering of an identifiable person. Christians have spoken out with a variety of voices on a wide range of political issues, but they have remained silent about a confirmation process that, in its pursuit of political ends, destroys real people. By this silence, Christians have departed from the teachings of their Lord, who condemned calumny as equivalent to murder.

"You have heard that it was said to those of ancient times, 'You shall not murder,' and 'whoever murders shall be liable to judgment.' But I say to you that if you are angry with a brother or sister, you will be liable to judgment; and if you insult a brother or sister, you will be liable to the council; and if you say, 'You fool', you will be liable to the hell of fire" (Matthew 5:21–22).

The confirmation process, especially for nominees to the Supreme Court, is out of hand. It has evolved from the Senate's constitutional responsibility to advise and consent to campaigns waged by interest groups to destroy the reputations of nominees. It is what Jesus condemned in the Sermon on the Mount. Christians of all political views should speak out against this, prophetically and with one voice.

Paul's Primer for Politics

C hristianity does not give us an agenda for American politics. It does not provide policy positions that we can identify with certainty as being Christian. What it does offer is an approach, a way of thinking about and engaging in politics, that while not issue specific, is highly relevant to our ability to live together as one nation, despite our strongly held differences. For me, one chapter in the New Testament has been especially helpful in describing how a Christian might approach politics. It is the twelfth chapter of Paul's Letter to the Romans, which I set out in full:

> *1* I appeal to you therefore, brothers and sisters, by the mercies of God, to present your bodies as a living sacrifice,

holy and acceptable to God, which is your spiritual worship.

2 Do not be conformed to this world, but be transformed by the renewing of your minds, so that you may discern what is the will of God—what is good and acceptable and perfect.

3 For by the grace given to me I say to everyone among you not to think of yourself more highly than you ought to think, but to think with sober judgment, each according to the measure of faith that God has assigned.

4 For as in one body we have many members, and not all the members have the same function,

5 so we, who are many, are one body in Christ, and individually we are members one of another.

6 We have gifts that differ according to the grace given to us: prophecy, in proportion to faith;

7 ministry, in ministering; the teacher, in teaching;

8 the exhorter, in exhortation; the giver, in generosity; the leader, in diligence; the compassionate, in cheerfulness.

9 Let love be genuine; hate what is evil, hold fast to what is good;

10 love one another with mutual affection; outdo one another in showing honor.

11 Do not lag in zeal, be ardent in spirit, serve the Lord.

12 Rejoice in hope, be patient in suffering, persevere in prayer.

13 Contribute to the needs of the saints; extend hospitality to strangers.

14 Bless those who persecute you; bless and do not curse them.

15 Rejoice with those who rejoice, weep with those who weep.

16 Live in harmony with one another; do not be haughty, but associate with the lowly; do not claim to be wiser than you are.

17 Do not repay anyone evil for evil, but take thought for what is noble in the sight of all.

18 If it is possible, so far as it depends on you, live peaceably with all.

19 Beloved, never avenge yourselves, but leave room for the wrath of God; for it is written, "Vengeance is mine, I will repay, says the Lord."

20 No, "if your enemies are hungry, feed them; if they are thirsty, give them something to drink; for by doing this you will heap burning coals on their heads."

21 Do not be overcome by evil, but overcome evil with good.

This passage, which is extraordinarily rich in content, is virtually a how-to manual for the Christian in politics. Different readers will emphasize different verses. Here are some thoughts that come to my mind as I read it.

LET'S KEEP POLITICS IN ITS PROPER PLACE

Politics can be a way of expressing our Christian values, but politics is not Christianity. As Paul tells us, "Do not be conformed to this world" (verse 2).

We have a strong inclination to let our politics determine our faith rather than the other way around. We have deep and long-held opinions about a range of political questions, certainly the hot-button social issues, such as abortion and gay marriage, but also economics, foreign policy, national defense, criminal justice and others. We may have come to these opinions in any of a number of ways. We may belong to a particular party because our parents were members; we may support low taxes because we have high incomes; we may support the death penalty because we have been victims of crime. Or it may be that we feel naturally drawn to liberal or conservative politics. The various ways we have come to our political opinions may have little or no connection to religion. When we vest our personal opinions with the trappings of religion, we make religion the servant of our politics. By confusing faith and politics, we become conformed to this world.

It is very tempting to use religion for our own purposes. Competing biblical citations are sometimes available for those who want to use them to support competing political arguments. For example, people arguing the pros and cons of increased defense spending could rely on the following quotations:

From Joel 3:9–10: "Prepare war, stir up the warriors. Let all the soldiers draw near . . . Beat your plowshares into swords, and your pruning hooks into spears; let the weakling say, 'I am a warrior.'"

From Micah 4:3: ". . . they shall beat their swords into plowshares, and their spears into pruning hooks; nations shall not lift up sword against nation, neither shall they learn war anymore."

Conservatives are not alone in their capacity to identify their political opinions with their faith. This can happen at any point on the philosophical spectrum. Consider what candidates of both political parties do on Sundays before elections. As a pro-life Republican, I have gone to evangelical Protestant churches, not really to worship but to appeal for votes. I recall a large, auditorium-like church as an example. I arrived after the service began, and the pastor introduced me as a good Christian who opposed abortion. I then proceeded to speak for a few minutes, using as a biblical text the passage from Deuteronomy in which God commands the people of Israel to "choose life." At the conclusion of my remarks, the pastor all but told the congregants that they should vote for me.

At the same hour when Republicans are speaking in predominantly white, evangelical Protestant churches, Democrats are making similar appeals in African American churches, and receiving similar kind words from the pulpit. The parties are different, and the issues have nothing in common, but the message is the same: To the extent possible without jeopardizing its tax-exempt status, this church supports this candidate. The candidate is using the church for political purposes, and the church is conforming itself to this world. It is just what Paul is telling Christians not to do—just what I should not have been doing when I was running for office.

Whether we are Republicans or Democrats, liberals or conservatives, it is important to recognize that our political opinions, no matter how strongly held, do not rise to the status of articles of faith. When considering faith and politics, we should keep some distance between the two.

NO ONE CORNERS THE MARKET ON TRUTH

Paul tells us "to think with sober judgment, each according to the measure of faith that God has assigned" (verse 3). He is speaking to

Christians in Rome, telling them that they are not all the same, but that they are "one body in Christ" (verse 4). They have different skills, different functions, different measures of faith and different ways of thinking, and with all those differences, they are one in Christ.

In verse 2, after telling Christians not to be "conformed to this world," Paul tells us to "be transformed by the renewing of your minds, so that you may discern what is the will of God—what is good and acceptable and perfect." God gave us brains and we are supposed to use them. To do the work of God in the world takes more than a good heart and a commitment of will. It takes renewal of the mind.

The old adage that polite conversation should not include talk of politics or religion is understandable because both subjects are so heavily laden with emotion that discussion can quickly turn to shouting. Blood is shed over politics, religion and the two in combination. But, as Paul tells us, Christianity is more than emotional. It engages and renews the mind. Christianity is not anti-intellectual. It is not a matter of feeling overcoming thinking.

Paul tells us that through renewing our minds, we "may discern what is the will of God." At times, the will of God comes in a flash, as it came to Paul on the road to Damascus. But Paul seems to realize that such revelations are the exception. More often, discerning God's will takes hard work. It requires us to think, to use our reason, to use judgment. Normally, we do not passively receive the will of God; we have to discern it. Paul speaks of the will of God as "what is good and acceptable and perfect." At the same time, he speaks of renewal of our minds—plural. Each of us has a mind, and each of us must use it. God wills what is perfect, but the perfect is a matter for the discernment of countless unique minds, and it transcends the discernment of any one mind. Each of us has a responsibility to think for himself. We cannot assume that God's will will be supplied to us from an external source—not by a pastor or church official, not by a television personality, not even by a revelation from God like Paul's on the road to Damascus.

Our responsibility is to think for ourselves about the implications of our faith and about the complex issues of government. Much of my time in the Senate was spent in the Finance Committee, which had jurisdiction over extraordinarily complex and important subjects, including taxation and health care policy. Some of the most able people in the Senate served on the Finance Committee, which was notably bipartisan in the way it functioned. When the committee wrote tax legislation, the hearing room was packed with brilliant people, all with expertise in the field of taxation. Each member had at least one tax expert on his staff. Then there was the staff of the Finance Committee, staffers on the Joint Committee of Taxation, representatives of the Treasury Department and, of course, a variety of lobbyists with knowledge of tax law. Every proposal for changing the Internal Revenue Code was examined in great detail. Would it provide desired incentives for improving the economy, and could its impact be quantified? Would it have negative consequences? Would it create loopholes? Was its benefit worth the cost to the treasury? The complexity of the tax code, the object of understandable complaint by most of us, is the result of very bright people trying to resolve exceptionally difficult and usually conflicting issues.

Tax law is the epitome of complexity, but it is not alone. My last two years in the Senate, the first two years of the Clinton presidency, were largely consumed by earnest bipartisan efforts to respond to the administration's attempts to reform America's health care system. After countless meetings, held virtually every day somewhere in the Capitol, the effort collapsed because even the brightest people could not anticipate the possible consequences proposed reforms would have on the delivery and cost of heath care.

Many times during my Senate years, constituents would say, in effect, "You're on the scene in Washington; we're not. You know what's going on; we don't. You tell us the answers." Such deference to government is never justified, for in a democracy we cannot afford to give the keys to the country to politicians, and then walk away. An ordinary citizen who takes the time to read a good newspaper can find out enough to have an informed opinion on almost every issue. The course of the country deserves careful thought by the public as well as by politicians.

This is even more so when one adds a religious dimension to issues of public policy. In that event, people of faith examine issues that are complex in their own right, such as taxation and health care, from their religious perspectives. The popular question "What would Jesus do?" can be difficult enough to contemplate with respect to everyday interpersonal relations. It is mind boggling when applied to the complex world of politics. Certainly, it requires a renewing of our minds if we are to come close to discerning the will of God.

RECOGNIZE OUR OWN LIMITATIONS

Legislating is a collective enterprise. Most pieces of legislation involve hosts of people with conflicting or cooperating interests. In 1985, when I became chairman of the Senate Commerce, Science and Transportation Committee, I visited one of my favorite senators, Russell Long, who had chaired the Finance Committee for years, to ask his thoughts on what makes an effective chairman. He said that it is important for the chairman to give every member of the committee a stake in some part of every important bill.

It is true that politics is the art of compromise, and that is how it should be. We have a large and diverse country, and the task of government is to hold various interests together. That was the idea behind our Constitution, with its intricate system of checks and balances: guarding against one region or interest running rough-shod over another and assuring that minorities have a right to be heard.

The American way is not one group having its way. No part of our country can have a monopoly of what is good for the whole. That is why we must be very careful in mixing religion in politics. The idea that God speaks to one group more than to others, or that one group uniquely represents the will of God, makes it im-possible to give outsiders the sense that they, too, are welcome participants in the life of our country.

Some people have asked me whether America is a Christian country. The answer must be no, for to call this a Christian coun-try is to say that non-Christians are of some lesser order, not full-fledged citizens of one nation.

Paul teaches us that even among practicing Christians, no one perfectly represents the totality of the faith. Each of us should think soberly "according to the measure of faith that God has as-signed"; therefore, we should not think of ourselves "more highly than [we] ought to think" (verse 3).

The problem with many conservative Christians is that they claim that God's truth is knowable, that they know it, and that they are able to reduce it to legislative form. Paul's message is quite different. We must "think with sober judgment," humbly acknowledging that whatever our thoughts, they are only "according to the measure of faith that God has assigned." God has given us different gifts, and God has given us different measures of faith. It is our responsibility to use these gifts "with sober judgment" to the best of our abilities in the service of God and our neighbors. That is the parable of the talents in which God gives people different assets but expects each person to take responsibility for putting those assets to use. God transcends our ability to understand him, much less our ability to impose our understanding of him on others through the power of government. On this earth, we see through a glass darkly, and at our best, we act in the light of that dim vision. Others have their own measures of faith. Others have their own perceptions of God's truth. They spend their own God-given talents according to their own lights. ". . . not all the members have the same function" (verse 4).

Immediately after telling us that practicing Christianity requires us to use our minds, Paul tells us how to think about ourselves. We are not to have an inflated self-regard. We are to think "with sober judgment," according to our apportioned measure of faith (verse 3). Once again, the emphasis is on using our God-given minds, critically and with good judgment, and that, in turn, entails recognizing our own limitations.

The finest forum I know for oratory is the floor of the United States Senate. It is a spacious and historic chamber, with an excellent sound system that carries one's voice to all corners of the room. Even better, most of the time few senators are on the floor, and even fewer are paying attention to what the speaker is saying, so any inhibitions an orator might have vanish with the pure, largely unmonitored sound of his own voice. The closest experience I have had to speaking in the Senate is singing in the shower. In my own imagination, what proceeds from my lips is magnificent.

As a group, members of the Senate are admirable individuals. They are bright, knowledgeable and energetic. But I would not count innate humility as one of their characteristics. To win their seats, senators engage in no-holds-barred election campaigns, and once elected, their daily lives consist of constant battles with one another over bills and amendments. Senators are sure of themselves, committed to their positions and assertive, and they enjoy the combat that is the essence of their job.

Supported by staff, flattered by lobbyists, whisked by capitol police into elevators reserved only for senators, nearly everything about a senator's life supports the inclination to "think of yourself more highly than you ought to think," especially while being transported to the farthest reaches of self-esteem by the splendid sound of your own rhetoric.

However, the pomposity that so much in a senator's life promotes cannot sustain itself because, as a practical matter, it is self-defeating. A senator who is carried away with his own importance would quickly lose the support of the people back home and would be ineffective in dealing with his colleagues. So senators, for the most part, are warm, regular people with the capacity to see the humor in what they are doing. There is something about shaking a corn-dog-encrusted hand at a county fair, or facing an irate constituent at a town hall meeting, or knowing that hundreds of thousands of constituents will go to the polls to vote against you that brings even the most self-satisfied politician down to earth.

It is equally humbling to know that the most grandiloquent words uttered on the Senate floor are likely to fall on deaf ears, or, in the frequent case of an empty chamber, on no ears at all. The fact is that other senators are not interested in your words. They are interested in how to accommodate their policy positions and the needs of their constituents with your legislation. It may be that they oppose your legislation, or that they can support it provided it can be amended to add some provision that is important to them. In no event are they there to be as impressed as you are by the sound of your voice.

Some of the best senators I knew were the most self-effacing. At the top of my list for effectiveness was Howard Baker, the Republican from Tennessee who was minority leader, then majority leader of the Senate, and subsequently served as chief of staff to President Reagan, then as United States ambassador to Japan. Baker has the smallest ego of anyone I have known in elective politics, and he is always ready with funny stories in which he is the object of his own humor. An example is his account of his trip to Knoxville, Tennessee, to announce his retirement from the Senate. For most of us, this would have been a grave and emotional occasion, certainly including philosophical thoughts about one's legacy in government. For Howard Baker, the telling of it centered on Wilbur Walker, Howard's elderly driver who, for decades, had driven a series of Republican leaders, including Robert Taft and Howard's father-in-law, Everett Dirksen. Wilbur was a taciturn gentleman who, to those of us who regularly passed him on the streets of Washington, seemed to drive considerably below the speed limit with Howard sitting next to him in the front of the leader's Lincoln Town Car.

On the way to Dulles Airport, Howard decided that he should break the news of his announcement so that Wilbur would not first learn of it on the radio. Wilbur's response was absolute silence, which lasted about thirty seconds, after which Wilbur turned to Howard and asked, "What is your last day?"

What makes the story funny, of course, is that the majority

leader of the Senate told it on himself. For all his lack of pomposity, I think because of it, Howard Baker was an enormously effective leader of the Senate. He knew when to push ahead and when to allow the Senate to move at its own pace. He was a master of friendly persuasion whose warm and reasonable way could bring senators to his point of view. He had strength without belligerence. He held together as a team Republican senators of very differing philosophies and temperaments, and he could work well and respectfully across party lines.

The understandable criticism of many Christians is that we seem so sure of ourselves, so certain that God is on our side and that we are on God's side. In our own imaginations, we know the truth, and it is absolute. So the tendency is to adopt an us-against-them mentality. Paul tells us we should not be "haughty" (verse 16). The dictionary definition of haughty is "disdainfully proud or overbearing: arrogant," which is exactly how we appear to others, especially when we transform our religious beliefs into a political agenda.

"LOVE ONE ANOTHER WITH MUTUAL AFFECTION; OUTDO ONE ANOTHER IN SHOWING HONOR"

In verse 10, Paul orders us to love one another with mutual affection, like it or not. Suppose we are seething inside, utterly contemptuous of another person. Everything he does rubs us the wrong way; everything he says grates on our nerves. In the world of politics, that is a very likely state of affairs. Then what? Paul's response could not be more clear: "[L]ove one another with mutual affection." "But," we say, "we can't love that person." Deep down in our hearts, we detest him. Regardless of how we feel, Paul tells us how we must act. We must act as though we love the other person. We must outdo one another in showing honor, even if we are gritting our teeth in doing it.

We might protest that going through the motions of loving someone when we don't feel like it is hypocritical. We pride ourselves on being straightforward, honest people who say what we think. If in the depths of our being we do not feel love for another person, we think it is duplicitous to pretend that we love him. If we find nothing good in another person, we think we are phony when we treat him with honor. The definition of hypocrisy is to say one thing and to do another. But the distinction between what we are and the way we act is false. We are what we do and say. We become people who love one another by acting as though we love one another.

In the heated world of politics, it is important to act as though we love one another, even where there is no underlying feeling of love. In the Senate, the language of affection and respect, even to the point of unctuousness, is the lubricant that allows the Senate to function.

My first debate on the Senate floor, on a long since forgotten topic, was against Senator Ed Muskie of Maine. A former presidential candidate and future secretary of state, Muskie was one of the most highly respected people in Washington. He was also known for his temper and his high-volume, red-in-the-face oratory on the Senate floor. Except for introducing myself to him on the day I was sworn in, I had never exchanged a word with Ed Muskie. As far as he was concerned, I was some unknown whippersnapper who had the gall to challenge one of his strongly held convictions. The debate was heated and the rhetoric loud, with Muskie shouting at me across the chamber. While I have no memory of the substance of the debate, I will never forget one phrase Muskie used amid the shouting and expressions of outrage. He called me "my very good friend from Missouri." He did not know me from Adam, and I had become his very good friend.

It struck me as odd at the time, but I quickly learned that Muskie's characterization of me was typical of Senatespeak. Senate rules state that one member is forbidden to verbally attack another, and he will be compelled to take his seat if he does so. To assure that debate is on the issues and is not personal, senators are supposed to speak by addressing the presiding officer and not other senators. But beyond these rules of decorum, senators regularly outdo each other in showing honor, heaping praise on colleagues whether it is warranted or not. A common manner of speaking is "No one has worked harder than my distinguished colleague to bring this bill to the floor," when, in fact, the distinguished colleague may have done little more than add his name as a cosponsor of the legislation.

Outdoing one another in showing honor is a long tradition in the Senate, but is has universal application. Organizations typically bestow long lists of awards during recognition dinners, and schools confer prizes and athletic letters, knowing that everyone responds well to being honored. The statement that we should go out of our way to honor people seems nothing more than everyday wisdom, the sort of thing we might read in the personal advice column of a newspaper.

It is good, commonsense advice, but in the Letter to the Romans, it is more than that. It is part of Paul's instruction on how to live the Christian life. In acting out our faith, Christians are told that they are expected to love one another with mutual affection, and to outdo one another in showing honor.

The requirement that we show honor definitely extends to fellow Christians with whom we disagree. After I wrote two newspaper opinion pieces stating that Christian conservatives should not control the Republican Party and do not speak for all Christians, a television reporter who interviewed me asked why I did not simply say that the conservatives are "nuts." He was inviting me to move in the opposite direction from Paul, to outdo myself in showing dishonor.

Moderates, who want their own views of religion and politics to be respected, have an obligation to respect the views of Christian conservatives, not just to secure their own place in public debate, but to fulfill Paul's mandate. Indeed, much as moderates might disagree with the particular policies advocated by conservatives, there is much in the conservative message that deserves their respect and support.

Moderate Christians might disagree with conservatives on issues of stem cell research, abortion and the appropriate circumstances for ending life support for the terminally ill. But moderates should both hear and honor the value that undergirds the conservative positions. Human life in whatever state, even at its most vulnerable, even at the farthest edges of life, is the gift of God and should be treated as such. Moderate Christians might disagree with conservatives on issues of church and state, on whether creationism should be taught in schools and the Ten Commandments posted in courthouses. But moderates should both hear and respect the values that undergird the conservative position: that religion is integral to all of life, that it is not a Sundays-only diversion, that it warrants inclusion in our daily lives. Moderate Christians might disagree with conservatives on the proposed constitutional ban on gay marriage. But moderates should both hear and respect the values that undergird the conservative position: that the joining together of a man and a woman in holy matrimony is instituted of God, and is to be honored among all people, and that human liberty does not include license to abandon the standards of sexual ethics.

Too often, moderates have treated conservative Christians with contempt, as though, in the word of the television interviewer, they are "nuts." In fact, they have a great deal to say to moderates, and they are worthy of our honor.

In politics, Paul's instruction means that even the most vehement argument on the most divisive, hot-button issue should take place in an atmosphere of mutual affection, where each side honors the views of the other. For those who practice politics as a career, the capacity to disagree in the context of friendship is not unusual. For ten years, I served in the Senate with my Missouri colleague Tom Eagleton. We are of opposite political parties, and we often disagreed on important issues, yet we were able to maintain a warm friendship that was well known to the people of our state. On many occasions, Missourians expressed to me appreciation that Eagleton and Danforth, quite different on the issues, got along with each other so well.

I have the impression that today's Senate is less inclined than in the past to encourage the kind of interpersonal relationships that transcend the controversies of the day. In the era of Lyndon Johnson and Everett Dirksen, senators are said to have gathered together for drinks at the end of the day. Now that Senate business often extends well into the evening, the cocktail hour may not be the appropriate custom to revive, but it did bring members together in an informal setting. The Senate gym continues to be a haven of bipartisan informality. I have a vivid recollection of earnestly discussing complex civil rights legislation in the gym with a colleague, both of us completely nude. It's difficult to be aggressive in such a circumstance.

Although mutual respect is a Senate tradition, it would be a mistake to believe that senators are an easygoing lot, always conducting their business with benign equanimity. The Senate is a place of legislative combat, where it is natural for tempers to flare. Late one night, during the final roll call vote of the day, a colleague became so enraged at something I had done that he asked me to go to the cloak room with him and "have it out," which I understood to mean duke it out. I said that he was free to go to the cloak room, but I was going home. My point is not that senators are unfailingly warm and happy-go-lucky, but that, by long tradition, they act toward one another with mutual affection, and they outdo one another in showing honor.

Short of reverting to the late afternoon cocktail hour, it would be possible for the Senate to take steps to encourage this mutual affection. In former times, members and their spouses gathered periodically in the Senate Caucus Room for dinners. That opportunity to get together socially, now largely abandoned, could be restored. During lunchtime, senators nearly always eat only with members of their own party. At least one day a week, they could make an effort to get together in bipartisan groups.

The intensity of politics pushes both politicians and the public away from the mutual affection Paul encourages. Step back and take the time to listen to how normal people express political opinions. This is the sort of thing I hear: "I hate Ted Kennedy!" "I hate Hillary Clinton!" "I hate Dick Cheney!" Perhaps this manner of expression is the product of the twenty-four hour news cycle. Perhaps it is a response to the harangues of apoplectic talking heads. Perhaps there is nothing new about it, and that's the way we have always talked about politics. Perhaps I never noticed. Whatever the case, it's the opposite of what Paul meant by mutual affection. It's the opposite of showing honor.

What Christianity brings to the arena of political conflict is a duty to act with mutual affection, a duty to show honor, even when we don't feel like doing so. It is a duty that extends to our most disagreeable foes.

ENGAGING THE ENEMY

Who is our enemy, and what are the rules of engagement for confronting him? For all the nonconfrontational emphasis of Romans 12, Paul is a realist. He recognizes what most of us take as the obvious: that we do have enemies, even very threatening enemies. We do not live in a make-believe land where everyone lives happily together. Paul goes so far as to call some of these enemies "evil" (verses 17 and 21). He assumes that enemies do more than create trouble. The enemies he speaks of persecute people. He speaks from his own experience as a former persecutor of Christians and an apostle to a persecuted church.

For Paul, the entry barrier to being considered an enemy was high: someone who is evil, a persecutor of the Church. For others, the barrier is much lower. I have known politicians who will not speak to people who, in the distant past, offended them. No matter that important issues are at stake, that the welfare of many constituents hangs in the balance, such politicians will not assist individuals or groups who opposed them in some previous election. Relatives of politicians can be even more unforgiving. Parents and wives are especially ready to hold grudges. I recently heard the father of an elected official say, "I can't bear it when people criticize my son."

To have hurt feelings is one thing. To take those feelings out in action is quite another. A notorious example of acting out grudges is the "enemies list" maintained by Richard Nixon's White House. The purpose of the list was to make certain that people who criticized or otherwise opposed the president received punishment.

The mixture of power and hypersensitivity to criticism can be dangerous, not only to the critic, but to the country. Dissenters who believe they will be punished for expressing themselves are unlikely to do so. Even if they are fearless about their own future, they will assume that a dissenting position will not get a hearing, and that expressing it is a waste of time. The considered judgment that should go into the making of public policy gives way to arrogance and, in the case of the Nixon presidency, to disaster.

In its day, the Nixon administration was described as the "imperial presidency." At one point, White House police were costumed in Gilbert and Sullivan–type uniforms in an apparent, and unwittingly comical, attempt to create a palacelike atmosphere. Quickly the new attire was abandoned in response to the loud guffaws of the American people.

David Boren was an example of a senator who did not hold grudges. To the contrary, he went out of his way to seek out would-be enemies and convert them into friends. A Democrat who consistently sought opportunities for bipartisan cooperation, he once introduced me to a business leader from Oklahoma who, he claimed, was one of his staunchest supporters. Boren later told me that early in his political career, the same business leader had actively backed his opponent. After that election, Boren, far from harboring ill feelings, made it a point to get to know the person, to find common ground, and to win a friend and supporter.

Every day the Senate is a battleground of hotly contested and constantly changing issues. Russell Long once advised me never to let the disagreements of one day carry over to the next, for I might need today's foe as tomorrow's ally. Again, the practical advice of a very practical politician is consistent with Paul's instruction that we "[l]ive in harmony with one another" (verse 16).

Paul's admonition that we live in harmony with one another seems like such pedestrian advice—the kind of thing we learned in Sunday school—that we might wonder if it is worth hearing yet again. It is, especially in today's religious and political climate. We have to hear this message again and again because with many of us, the stronger our faith, the more strident we become. In the twenty-first century, no one is persecuting us, but we adopt the language of victimization, claiming that those who disagree with us are enemies of the faith.

Paul's instructions to the Romans contrast sharply with the tone of twenty-first century American politics. "Bless those who persecute you; bless and do not curse them" (verse 14) contrasts with a four-page single-spaced letter I recently received from a professed Christian. Its subject was homosexuality, and with citations from the books of Leviticus and Revelation, it imposed a curse on me for saying the Republican Party should back off its recent emphasis on the gay marriage issue. Strangely, after consigning me to an eternity in hell, the anonymous writer concluded his letter, "Have a nice day. Bob." Admonitions not to "repay anyone evil for evil" (verse 17) and "never avenge yourselves" (verse 19) seem to have no bearing in today's highly partisan political conflict. "[I]f your enemies are hungry, feed them" (verse 20) has had no effect on a Senate where the two parties eat lunch in separate rooms.

The twelfth chapter of Paul's Letter to the Romans seems out of touch with the reality of today's politics. No doubt it was just as out of touch with the reality of first-century Rome, or Paul would not have written it. That is just the point. It is not a message for everyone. These are instructions to Christians on how they should relate to a world given to meanness and to fracturing.

RECONCILIATION DEPENDS ON US

"[S]o far as it depends on you, live peaceably with all" (verse 18). That is Paul's advice to Roman Christians of the first century and American Christians of the twenty-first century. Just as Paul understands that in the real world we will have enemies, so he suggests that, despite our best intentions, some things in life are beyond our control. We may want to live in peace with our neighbors and work out whatever differences we have, but sometimes our neighbors are not interested in reaching accommodation with us. All of us have known people who make no effort to be reasonable. A friend once described a very combative lawyer by saying, "He eats glass for breakfast."

In affairs among nations, it is sometimes impossible to live peaceably, no matter how fervently we may pray for peace. In the 1940s, it was not possible for the United States to live peaceably with Nazi Germany. But living peaceably is the goal, and so far as it depends on us, that is what Paul says we should try to do.

Many Americans believe that something has gone terribly wrong with our politics. They say as much when they tell pollsters that our country is on the wrong track and that they lack confidence in our government's ability to address major issues. They do not believe that either political party speaks for them, and they are offended by the relentless nastiness of what they see on television and hear during election years. Many times, ordinary citizens have expressed to me a sense of being powerless. They do not like the tone of politics, but they do not know what they can do to change it.

Paul challenges Christians to assume responsibility for doing their part to live peacefully in a world in conflict. But when Christians claim special knowledge of God's truth, when they advance wedge issues, when they divide America between "people of faith" and their "enemies," Christians become not the means of peace but the cause of conflict. In that case, Christians are far from being powerless. They are powerful contributors to what has gone wrong in American politics.

If Christians have the power to contribute to what is wrong, they have the power to right the wrong. They have the power to substitute the ministry of reconciliation for the strategy of divisiveness. Where Christians in politics often have been notable for their hubris, claiming that they speak for God, they can, instead, be notable for their humility, acknowledging that God's truth is greater than anything they can hope to express. Where Christians have championed wedge issues that divide Americans, they can substitute a search for common ground on which Americans might unite to address common challenges. Where Christians have polarized our politics, pushing us to ideological extremes, they can rebuild our political center and help bring us together. Where Christians have been quick to anger, they can show honor to their adversaries and bring civility to our politics.

"[S]o far as it depends on you." Well, a united America does depend on us. It is the responsibility of people who follow Jesus. It is not a political agenda. It is the ministry of reconciliation.

Acknowledgments

For most of the eighteen years that our family attended St. Alban's Church in Washington, D.C., the rector was the Reverend Francis H. Wade, the most consistently insightful preacher I have known. At least one of his sermons, and probably more, concerned the central point of this book and has had a lasting influence on the way I think about the relationship of faith to politics. He preached on God's purpose of healing a fractured world and said that the word "religion" is derived from the same root as the word "ligament," that which binds together different parts of the body. I have borrowed from Frank Wade's sermon many times, including as mentioned in the chapter "Blessed Are the Peacemakers," in a meeting with the clergy of Sudan. My concern about the way Christians have used wedge issues in politics directly relates to

Acknowledgments

Frank's message. Intentional divisiveness contradicts the very meaning of religion.

My friend and former bishop, Hays Rockwell, encouraged me to write this book and offered helpful comments on an early manuscript. He, too, has had a profound influence on my thinking. Several years ago, I sought his advice on how to conduct the funeral of a very good person who might not have been a Christian. He told me that how a person lives is more important than what a person says about religion. He then spoke of John's Gospel, paraphrasing Jesus as saying that there are many large, inviting rooms in his father's house. It is an important thought about an inclusive church that I have included in this book.

Nearly two years ago, I left public life to spend more time with my wife, Sally. It turned out that I have spent much of that time in the silence of writing. She has been wonderfully understanding and supportive, and of great practical help in my effort. "Family Values" draws on the experiences of Sally and our five children, Eleanor Ivie, Mary Stillman, D. D. Burlin, Jody Root and Tom Danforth.

Colleagues who have worked with me on various subjects have shared their memories of events and have reviewed relevant parts of the manuscript. They include Ambassador Richard Holbrooke, who was crucial in America's effort to save the lives of Cambodians, and ambassadors Robert Oakley and Michael Ranneberger, two outstanding diplomats who have been deeply involved in Sudan. The Reverend Michael Perry, OFM, has shared with me his experience with church-related peacemaking efforts in Africa, and Nicholas Rostow, now vice chancellor and general counsel at the State University of New York, has been generous with his encyclopedic knowledge of world conflict.

Acknowledgments

I am grateful to William Neaves, M.D., president of the Stowers Institute, Professor Martin Marty of the University of Chicago, Professor Michael Graetz of Yale Law School and Judge Guido Calabresi for reading all or parts of the manuscript and giving me excellent advice on how to improve it. Guido was my teacher at Yale Law School and ever since has been my mentor and friend.

Of course, the opinions I express as well as any errors in the text are my responsibility, not theirs.

Throughout my public life, I was blessed with the help of excellent people who worked on my staff. They are bright, able and highly principled, and they deserve credit for any good I might have done while in office. For twenty-two of my years as attorney general of Missouri and U.S. senator, the glue that held my staff together was my friend since childhood and my administrative assistant, Alex Netchvolodoff. Any acknowledgment for anything I have ever done must recognize his selfless contribution. People who were with me in my Senate office and who were responsible for the events I describe in this book were extraordinarily helpful in sharing their recollections and reviewing my work. Particularly, I appreciate the help of Janet Brown, Tracy Kaye, Peter Leibold, Allen Moore, Genny Nicholas and Mark Weinberger.

Martha Fitz has been involved in every aspect of this book, from researching facts to typing all stages of the manuscript and offering her good advice on content. Since I left the Senate, she has been my right arm and loyal associate.

I am grateful for the encouragement I have received from my colleagues at Bryan Cave LLP, both in the writing of this book and in all my activities that do not relate to the normal work of a law firm. They have been consistently supportive, and they have made one of our fine associates, Jason Hall, available to assist me with research. I am proud to be their partner, and I am appreciative of Jason's help.

Robert Barnett has ably represented me in connection with this book. Everyone at Viking who has been a part of this effort has been most helpful, especially my editor, Carolyn Carlson. Her support has been steady and her judgment invaluable.

Early in the process, Carolyn and I decided on the title, *Faith and Politics*, a decision that has left me with lingering doubts. It seems a bit pretentious, as though it implies that this is a definitive statement of how faith relates to politics. I hope the text makes it clear that no such implication is intended and that all of us should approach the connection of faith to politics with great humility. This book states a point of view, and nothing more.

It is healthy for America that in recent months astute observers have expressed their own points of view about faith and politics. This subject will benefit from a good public airing. But a public airing depends on more than the few who write newspaper columns or books. It depends on the active engagement of many people who will think and speak about the issue. My purpose is to help stimulate widespread public discussion. For this reason, the success of this book will depend more on the readers than on the writer.